Chinchilla Handbook

Edmund Bickel

TRANSLATED BY U. ERICH FRIESE

Photography: BLACK AND WHITE PHOTOS by Dr. Herbert R. Axelrod, Chinchilla Association of America, Bernie Crampton, Michael Gilroy, Dr. Grzimek (Zoological Garden, Frankfurt), National Chinchilla Breeders Association (New York), and Willis D. Parker. COLOR PHOTOS by Dr. Herbert R. Axelrod, Michael Gilroy, J. A. Wilkinson (Valan Photos), and John Zeinert.

Contents

Preface to the Fifth Edition

"Breeding chinchillas is an art as well as a business."

[Willis D. Parker]

On my way home from the first exhibition of fur-bearing animals I ever visited, at the Munich Exhibition Park in the fall of 1928, I thought about whether it would be possible to breed South American chinchillas. After all, at that time their pelts were worth a small fortune. I remember, for instance, a magazine photograph of a coat made of Boliviano pelts with a price of half a million gold marks.

At that time — now over half a century ago — the public's focal point was on silver foxes, but mink and beaver were also on display.

Since I have always had an inclination toward animals, I began to develop an interest in this new type of business venture, in a — at that time — rather difficult economic climate. I started to review the relevant literature, and most notably I read the small booklet *The economics of breeding fur-bearing animals* by Edward W. A. Stein and Dr. Adolf Priesner. My particular attention was drawn to the last page, where it was said of the chinchilla: "As a point of interest it should be mentioned that attempts are already being made in America to breed true chinchillas; the incredible prices paid for pelts from this small animal, which combines fertility with modest food requirements, virtually demand this. It is understood that only high alpine regions can be

5

The standard gray chinchilla is bred very widely in many parts of Europe, Canada, United States, and South America. It is also the chinchilla you will find often in pet shops.

used for breeding these animals. Reliable information about the economic success of such activities is not known."

I have spent many years collecting, examining, and reviewing reference material about chinchillas. The result is this book, which now appears in its fifth edition. In conjunction with this is also a modest anniversary: It has been exactly two decades since this book was published in its first edition as the very first text in the German language on this particular subject.

Its objective is to convey to those interested in chinchillas as much information as possible to spare them disappointments and losses. Even the experienced chinchilla breeder may take advantage of this book and find useful suggestions in it. After all, there is no such thing as a "perfect" method for keeping chinchillas: the learning process never stops.

Before you make a decision to start breeding chinchillas, I must be permitted to make a few well-meant suggestions. Even when you are being assured, when visiting a chinchilla farm or similar facility, that it is very easy to breed chinchillas, the hard facts of reality are such that several prerequisites have to be fully met:

— One has to be willing to spend sufficient time daily, throughout the entire year, with the animals. This even means foregoing vacations when there is no reliable person around to take over during this period.

— The cages and breeding room must be kept clean at all times, because pelts from a dirty facility will lose in value.

— The breeder has to have the financial means and time not only to properly set up his facility, but also to allow it to be enlarged and still be adequately manageable.

— It must be kept in mind that much time and money will have to be put into the facility until chinchilla breeding brings a profit. Anyone who claims that breeding chinchillas can bring quick profits either does not know what he is talking about or is out to deceive you.

All this is certainly not encouraging to anyone interested in breeding these animals. In fact, it is not intended to be, but it can stop you from making a hasty decision.

It is strongly recommended that anyone wishing to get into chinchilla breeding visit as many breeding facilities and chinchilla farms as possible. Not only does this convey some ideas about the quality of animals available, but it will also allow you to learn what poor animals look like as well as those of good quality. Other information is also obtained at the same time, most notably the prevailing price range of breeding stock available. Anyone who can afford to travel and is competent in a foreign language could certainly benefit from visiting chinchilla breeding farms in Europe and North America.

An even better way to gain a good working knowledge about chinchillas is to work in a large, well-established facility for a few weeks without pay. This can bring much valuable hands-on experience.

One thing is certain: those who have a particular inclination and tenacity for breeding chinchillas can develop a fascinating hobby into a solid and lucrative trade. This is evident in many chinchilla breeding farms that have been in existence for many years and have brought prestige and prosperity in their owners.

Nevertheless, it must be pointed out that breeding chinchillas has also brought financial losses and disappointment to some people because they have chased after a dream without having sufficient knowledge of what is involved in such a venture.

Once again, I would like to conclude this preface by expressing my gratitude to the publisher for our successful amicable cooperation, which has now lasted for two decades. Similarly, I would like to express my sincere thanks to Dr. Theodor Haltenorth, the author of the newly established systematics of chinchillas, and to Prof. Dr. Helmut Kraft, Medical Animal Clinic of the Veterinary College, Munich, advisor on questions in his area of professional competence. I am also greatly indebted to Mr. Gerhard Schreiber, publisher and editor of the journal *Chinchilla Post*, for his very experienced advice.

Edmund Bickel
Munich, 1977

Preface to the Sixth Edition

Edmund Bickel died on 15 March 1981, at the age of nearly 82 years. He was a kind, helpful, and open man who had given his love to animals, especially to chinchillas, which he himself bred in North America during the early 1930's.

Therefore, it was only natural that he, on the basis of his hands-on experience with this species, together with his bibliographic research of foreign publications on this subject, wrote the first book (in 1956) in German on chinchilla breeding, *South American chinchillas, their care and breeding*. This happened at just the right moment, because from 1952 on, chinchilla breeding started to spread in Germany, yet nobody knew how to keep this animal, much less how to feed and breed it.

His contributions in the form of German translations of American and Swedish source material in the *Deutschen Pelztierzuechter* and in the *Chinchilla Post* were also decisive factors for the development of chinchilla breeding. Moreover, Edmund Bickel worked on the *Chinchilla Post* since it was established in 1956. There was indeed a cordial bond between us.

Similarly, he also brought pen to paper — in other journals — on behalf of chinchilla breeding, and he voiced a warning early on against commercial excesses and condemned blind profit motives.

Edmund Bickel's word has had a decisive influence upon chinchilla breeding in Europe, which has become greatly indebted to him. For this he deserves the gratitude of all German and other European chinchilla breeders as well as their perpetual, honorable respect.

Gerhard Schreiber
Munich, 1983

Biology of Chinchillas

When I visited Richard Gloeck in his wholesale furrier establishment in Leipzig in 1931, it was the first opportunity for me to see, side-by-side, several pieces of the three types of chinchilla pelts being commercially traded at the time. Mr. Gloeck, then known as the "Chinchilla King," was so kind as to pass on to me all relevant information about these pelts. His vast experience and substantial knowledge strongly suggest that the systematic arrangement of chinchillas based on his work should be accepted, even though it may not necessarily be in total compliance with current generally accepted scientific classifications. To verify the early Gloeck-based work is virtually no longer possible since the animals have become nearly extinct in their native countries. Consequently, material needed for anatomical comparisons is no longer available in sufficient quantity.

Classification

Nevertheless, those pelts shown to me displayed such unmistakably distinct differences that I have come to the conclusion that they prove the existence of three distinct types of chinchillas. Each type has a distinctive size, hair length, and tail length. It has been clearly proven that the currently captive-bred *Chinchilla lanigera,* referred to as *"velligera,"* and *Chinchilla chinchilla,* referred to as *"brevicaudata,"* are indeed two independent species. The two scientific names *velligera* and *brevicaudata* are, according to the currently valid nomenclature, out of date. Yet, since chinchilla breeders in the Old and New World are still using these generally, they are being maintained in this book in order to avoid misunderstandings. On the other hand, a name does not

A Brevicaudata female chinchilla.

appear to be in current use for the largest species. It is possibly identical with *C. brevicaudata* variety *major* as listed by Trouessart (Berlin, 1897), but that name is no longer listed in the standard mammal catalogs, which list only *C. lanigera* and *C. brevicaudata*. Here it will be called *C. chinchilla chinchilla*, with the *"brevicaudata"* type called *C. c. boliviana*.

I have discussed this particular topic already in *Der Zoologische Garten*, N.F. IV 1931, pages 63 ff. Since there was no objection at the time to my proposals, I am quoting them here. I hope that there may someday be an opportunity to obtain valid evidence for my assertions.

Synopsis of Chinchilla Classifications

Scientific Name	Common Names
Chinchilla chinchilla chinchilla	Royal Chinchilla Chinchilla Real Greater Short-tailed Chinchilla
Chinchilla chinchilla boliviana	Brevicaudata Blue Bolivian Chinchilla Boliviano Lesser Short-tailed Chinchilla "Indiana" type
Chinchilla lanigera	Velligera Lanigera Chilena Coastal Chinchilla Long-tailed Chinchilla "La Plata" type "Costina" type "Raton" type

1) The largest, most attractive and rarest species of chinchillas is the **Royal Chinchilla** or **Chinchilla Real,** as this species is called in South America (the scientific name is *Chinchilla chinchilla chinchilla*). Since "real" can both mean "regal or royal" and "true or genuine," this should be mentioned here. The fur trade referred to the Chinchilla Real as "Royal Chinchilla." In this context — and for the sake of accuracy — it must also be mentioned that furriers usually distinguished between "true" and "bastard/hybrid" chinchillas, which is, however, misleading. The latter term needs to be elaborated on. The form later introduced as the Royal Chinchilla by the fur trade and for which the French name "Chinchilla de Perou" is used is also different, since it probably originated in the Cordillera Real (often translated as "Royal Mountains") in Bolivia, which is from the range of *C. chinchilla boliviana*.

It is common practice to list sizes when animals are described, yet this was not possible for this species since all support data are no longer available. According to my memory, these pelts were about one-fifth larger than the other types discussed below; in other words, in comparison to those they were conspicuously larger. In coloration this species was not distinct from the other two, but the hair was longer and exceptionally silky, which gave those few pelts that I saw an unusual beauty. When blown against the hair it would "flow" more than those of the other two types. Another distinguishing characteristic was the conspicuously short and bushy tail. The tail is usually a reliable feature to tell the three types apart. There is a general rule which must be remembered: the smaller the species, the relatively longer the tail.

Whether the Chinchilla Real still exists in the wild or whether it belongs among the extinct animal species can not be stated with certainty. The Swede Martin Nilsson, the founder of the later nationalized Argentinian breeding facility Criadero Nacional de Chinchillas, Abra Pampa, Province Jujuy, and whom I believe to be a reliable source, told me at our meeting in 1931 that he had a pair of this species that had been caught in the wild. He also advised me that the nutritional requirements were similar to that of the Bolivian type (*"brevicaudata"*), but it required less green food and would produce only one litter per year, the female giving birth to a single young. This is all I have been able to ascertain about this species in the more than four decades during which I have been gathering data about these animals. Therefore, only two facts can be determined: that the fur trade knew the true Royal Chinchilla, and that a reliable witness had indeed kept this species. The pelts from this species have always been by far the rarest, and because of their beauty they were the most highly prized. Yet the fur trade, in its listings of chinchilla pelts, did not distinguish between pelts from Royal Chinchillas and Bolivianos ("*brevicaudata*"), but did so in their price. Presumably this was due to the fact that the small number of pelts was insufficient to establish separate assortments.

2) The **Blue Bolivian Chinchilla,** in Spanish the **Boliviano.** The scientific name for this species (actually now considered a subspecies of the Royal) is *Chinchilla chinchilla boliviana,* also referred to as "*brevicaudata.*"

When compared to the third type, *C. lanigera,* this one is clearly distinguishable. It is smaller than the preceding species, the Royal, and its hair is somewhat shorter, yet it now produces the most attractive, densest, and largest pelts for the market. Its ears are roundish and only sparsely covered with hairs along the outer margins. According to the literature, this type obtains a maximum size of 30 cm, with a tail length of 13 cm (20 cm, including hair). The tail is characterized by the presence of strong, dense, bristle-like hairs along the sides. It bends upward when the animal is sitting. A running or jumping animal extends its tail, using it as a rudder. Here it must be pointed out that the above measurements are really only indicators, since often substantial size variations are common among chinchillas. Females are generally somewhat longer than bucks, and they are also usually less timid.

Boliviano pelts were always less common in the fur

trade than the smaller Chilena pelts. For that reason the former would also fetch a higher price than the latter. Richard Gloeck reports that the Boliviano pelts had perhaps a 20% share of the market. Even today the overall population of this type — usually referred to as Brevicaudata by breeders — is hardly larger than a few thousand animals. Just as the Chinchilla Real is probably a distincly high alpine occupant, the Boliviano is also found at altitudes between 2,000 and 4,000 m. Today Brevicaudata (*C. c. boliviana*) is rarely kept in the United States; instead, the vast population of animals kept there belong to *C. lanigera*, usually called the Velligera, discussed later. During the 1950's, breeding Brevicaudata was also tried at several localities — and at great expense — in Germany, but for unknown reasons this was not successful.

Here it is also relevant to make some reference to the type referred to as **Indiana** by the fur trade. Mr. Gloeck was unable to tell me whether this was a valid species or subspecies, or possibly only a geographically limited type (strain or race). He thought that these might have been animals that lived along the eastern slopes of the Cordilleras. In any event, "Indiana" is a pelt quality designation. Pelts from these animals are generally of inferior quality, although in size they correspond to those of Bolivianos. Since their color has a yellowish or brownish tone, furriers can not use them for top-quality fur apparel. Therefore, they are often "blended" (treated with a sponge and dyes in order to make them look more attractive). It is, however, not possible to remove the yellowish or brownish tinge completely. Yellow toning is often an indicator of the age of fur apparel. Light, especially sunlight, tends to discolor chinchilla pelts (as indeed all gray pelts) to a yellowish tone over the course of time, and such pelts lose some of their appeal and decline in value. This is today clearly visible in apparel made from chinchilla pelts at the turn of the century. Therefore, it is imperative that chinchilla pelts are not exposed to direct sunlight if they are to keep their value.

When, on behalf of some financial backers, I undertook a breeding attempt with three adult pairs of Brevicaudata in the swampy "10,000 Lakes" area in Minnesota in the spring of 1931, the prevailing conditions were not particularly favorable for this project to succeed. The area is only about 300 m above sea level, with a climate characterized by considerable temperature extremes, with summer temperatures of about 40°C, while the nights were cool. During the winter the temperatures would fall as low as -40°C. It goes without saying that the animals, which originated from Martin Nilsson's Argentine breeding farm, Abra Pampa, were accommodated in a wooden building.

The breeding farm at Abra Pampa, established by Nilsson, was described in *Der Deutschen Pelztierzuechter* (1 July 1930) in an illustrated article entitled "Criadero Nacional de Chinchillas." I had translated this article, and at this point a summary may be of interest to the reader:

"This farm [now allegedly nationalized by the Argentinian government] is located about 21 kilometers from the railroad station Abra Pampa, at the base of a small mountain at the edge of enormous pampa, at an elevation of nearly 4,000 m above sea level.

"The chinchillas are kept in enclosures with dimensions of 4 m x 1 m x 1.2 m; three of these enclosures are joined into a larger one. Each of them contains a hut, similar to fox huts, but substantially smaller. A 1.5-m-long burrow tube (30 cm in diameter) is attached to this hut and leads to the nest box inside the hut. The ground of the enclosure is covered by a pile of rocks, because the animals like to hide among them or perch on top of them. There is also sand for bathing in the enclosure as well as on the floor of the nest box. This sand is of a particular type found in the nearby mountains and carried down by donkeys. The sand serves to maintain and protect pelt quality. Wild-caught chinchillas that have a fur of mediocre quality can hardly be recognized after some time on the farm; this improvement is attributed to the favorable influence of the sand.

"The chinchillas are fed once a day during the evening. Their food consists generally of different types of hay, carrots, and cacti, the usual food of these animals in the wild; however, vegetables such as lettuce, fruit, grass, and barley also make a good diet. Water is unnecessary, and even when placed inside the enclosure the animals will not touch it. This farm was established in 1927 by Martin Nilsson."

At that time it was barely known that Chapman actually had started breeding the long-tailed Chilean Chinchillas (or Chilenas), which are now common, four years before Nilsson started his breeding facility. Attempts to breed Brevicaudatas or Bolivianos, which because of the size and beauty of their pelts are far more valuable than Chilenas, were started many years ago in North America and Europe. For obvious reasons I still have strong affinities for Bolivianos; it was the first type I got involved with. So far I have still not been able to find an explanation for why a number of German breeders have failed with Bolivianos even though they had invested much time and effort in this. As far as I know, the Bolivianos started to die off gradually, although in my experience these animals are not difficult to breed; after all, all three pairs given to me produced progeny. I can also not understand why there are breeding facilities for Bolivianos in Argentina and Chile and possibly also in other South American republics, yet little information is available about these facilities, such as how large they are and whether or not they sell breeding stock, and there are no details about the amounts of pelts produced.

According to Dr. Juan Grau, Santiago, Chile, who runs a breeding facility established with wild-caught breeding stock and who is known as an authority, Brevicaudata still occurs as a wild form in the Peruvian, Bolivian, and Chilean Andes. It is supposed to be particularly abundant along the Argentine side of the Andes, in the areas opposite Antofagasta and Cociapo. There this species lives in burrows at elevations from 2,700 m to 4,000 m above sea level.

3) *Chinchilla lanigera,* also referred to as **Chilena, Long-tailed chinchilla, Velligera,** Coastal Chinchilla, and Chinchilla da Costa.

It is this species that in Chile used to occur all the way down to the coastal regions. As reported by Frederico Albert in 1900, early authors wrote: "...that the numbers of these animals used to be extraordinarily large, and that they would run around and underneath mules, and a traveler could see thousands of these animals during a single day's journey." At the time when this early monograph (intended but not heeded as a conservation warning) was published these animals had already become rather scarce in their natural habitat. "They are still occurring in sizable numbers in the Administrative District Vallenar, but in all other regions there is bitter disappointment about the frightening decline.... In many regions they are already completely exterminated, as for instance in the provinces of Antofagasta and Tauca."

According to physician Dr. Juan Grau, who had extensively studied the distribution, behavior, and nutrition of chinchillas in their natural habitat, *C. lanigera* still occurs (despite continuous hunting pressure) on nearly all coastal mountains from Antofagasta to Ranca-

A beautiful chinchilla of the Lanigera breed.

gua at elevations from 360 to 2300 m above sea level. It occupies areas uninhabitated by humans. Individual colonies occur like islands, surrounded by roads, railway lines, and densely populated regions. Dr. Grau operates a breeding facility in central Chile established with animals caught in the wild under collecting permits from the Chilean Government. According to his observations such wild-caught stock is very resistant to environmental extremes and other adversities. He reports, for instance, a colony he knows at an elevation of 1370 m above sea level where the temperature drops from 21°C during the day to below freezing at night. In the summer the mercury climbs during the day to 30°C in the shade and drops back down to 7°C at night. Consequently, the chinchillas in that region are exposed to considerable temperature extremes.

Due to extensive breeding in North America, *Chinchilla lanigera* is now the common species. The word "lanigera" translates into "bearing a woolen coat," yet chinchillas do not have a woolen coat, but instead one consisting of hair. Therefore, "wool bearing" is also not a distinguishing characteristic. All the species or types have essentially the same hair. This species is often called the "Velligera."

Brehm gives a maximum size of 35 to 40 cm (⅓ of this is tail) for this small Chilean species and states that it is much smaller than *C. brevicaudata* (= *C. c. boliviana*). He lists northern and central Chile as the range for this species, and further states that hair length on the back of these animals is 2 cm, along the flanks and sides 3 cm. Brehm does not provide any specifics about the hair of Brevicaudata, which — in any event — is longer. With the same smokiness and same color quality for both, the pelts of Brevicaudata are superior to that of the Chilena in size and hair length and consequently more valuable. Both species occur in light, medium, and dark types. Similarly, there are also conspicuously large as well as very small animals. Again, females are generally slightly larger than bucks. Presumably both species lived originally side-by-side in the same area. Whether this has led to hybrids is not known. *C. lanigera* is characterized by the larger and more elongated ears, which are weakly covered with hairs along the inside. This gives them an appearance reminiscent of hares and rabbits, thus the German name "hare mice" for the species.

The following measurements were given by Frederico Albert in his monograph for an adult animal (sex not indicated):

From tip of nose to base of tail	28-40 cm
Tail length	13-16 cm
Ear length	4.5-5 cm
Ear width	3-3.5 cm
From fetter to tip of nails	5-6 cm
Width of forefoot area	2.5-3 cm
Length of forefoot nails	0.2-0.25 cm
Length of hind foot nails	0.35-0.4 cm
Length of whiskers	10-13 cm

Figures like these can of course only be accepted as indicators, since, as already mentioned, there is considerable size disparity between individual animals.

The fur trade, as well as Brehm, has used the term "hybrid" chinchilla for *C. lanigera,* but since it is misleading, it was purposely omitted from our list of names. This term may have arisen from the appearance of pelts that looked like they had come from crosses (hybrids). It must also be quite unequivocally noted that so-called hybrids have nothing whatsoever to do with Brevicaudata X Velligera crosses. These were indeed successfully produced in North America and Europe some years ago, but they are of only zoological interest because they confirm the close relationship between these two species. They have no economic value since they can not be used for further breeding. If the original male in such crosses was a Brevicaudata, then the F1 progeny males are supposed to be fertile. If the male was a Velligera and the female a Brevicaudata, then the entire progeny from such mating is supposed to be infertile. The external appearance of such crosses is reminiscent of Brevicaudata in head shape, while the body is smaller. There are no economic advantages in such crosses, not even in pelt quality, since thoroughbred Brevicaudata are from the start superior in pelt characteristics to *Chinchilla lanigera* of identical quality due to their size and the presence of longer hair. Apart

A chinchilla of the La Plata type.

from the fact that nature has already intervened, it is also pointless to cross these two species, because pelt sorters have enough difficulty already picking out matching pelts from the scarce pelt offerings brought to the market.

De Chant (deceased 1956) established three different types of Velligera, *C. lanigera*. He referred to these as La Plata, Costina, and Raton. Each of these has its own peculiar characteristics, so it may be relevant to describe these here.

The La Plata Type

These animals can be distinguished from the two other types by a better developed musculature and heavier bone structure. They look more roundish or compact, with a short, wide head, large distance from one ear to the other, a relatively straight dorsal line. The shoulders are often as wide as the chest and rump. The ears are short and nearly round.

In De Chant's opinion, pelt density and (in many specimens) the larger size are the most valuable characteristics of this type. In all other characteristics, however, this type falls behind those of the other two types. In the La Plata type the hair is usually a bit too long, especially along the flanks. The prevailing color shades are medium, medium light, and light; occasionally there is also a light brown or yellowish tinge.

The Costina Type

When compared with the La Plata type, this type is weaker in musculature and bone structure, with the most distinctive feature being the longer hind legs. The fore legs are shorter, placed closer together, and the shoulders are narrower, so that it weighs substantially less despite its equal size. The vertebral column is more arched, the neck line sometimes very deep, forming a slight hump on the back of the animal. When viewed directly from the front, the head has a V-shape, the nose is pointed, and the distance between the ears is rather wide. The ears as such are long and are positioned at an angle of about 45 degrees. Pelts from this type often exhibit a better color than those of the La Plata type. Costina chinchillas are usually more elongated, and there-

A chinchilla of the Costina type.

fore they supply longer and narrower pelts. The hair in Costinas conforms more to the needs of the fur trade; it is very even in length, except in the back of the neck and over the shoulders up to the middle of the back; there it is shorter.

The Raton Type

In body structure this type appears to be reminiscent of the La Plata type. The nose is as pointed as in Costinas, but the ears are positioned very close together and rather horizontal. They are distinctly small animals that on the average are about a third or a quarter smaller than the La Plata type. The pelt of this type used to be the most attractive, but through crosses with the other two types it has gradually deteriorated.

These details are useful to the breeder because, when selecting his breeding stock and particular pairs or polygamous breeding groups, he should orient his selection toward the pelt characteristics of the individual types in order to achieve a particular breeding objective.

BIOLOGICAL CHARACTERS

There used to be little information about the longevity of chinchillas. One of the first bits of reliable information was provided by Richard Gloeck, who had obtained an approximately 2-year-old *C. lanigera* buck in Chile and taken it back to Leipzig. The animal lived for more than 11 years in a wire cage. Since then it has become known that chinchillas reach a (for rodents) relatively substantial age in excess of 20 years. This is in strong contrast to many other rodent species. For instance, Golden Hamsters get barely older than 1½ to 2 years; the females give birth to young after a gestation period of only 16 days (litter size, six to eight young), and after about seven litters they are already infertile and old. Yet experience has shown that chinchilla females remain fertile until they are quite old. For instance, in a Canadian breeding farm one of the most attractive females was 17 years old and weighed more than 1 kg. It had a very dense pelage and produced two litters every year with two or three young each. The same establishment also had a buck that was still copulating successfully at an age of 18 years and finally died at 21 years of age. But chinchillas designated for skinning are usually not kept beyond the first seven to ten months, when the first pelt maturity is reached. On the other hand, the fact that these animals do get quite old may persuade some breeders to retain high quality animals as studs for longer periods of time.

Velligera is always superior to Brevicaudata in litter sizes. For the former it is advisable not to use a higher reproductive base line than 100% per breeding per year, even when the more successful breeding farms are able to produce a progeny of six young and even more from a single female within two years. As reported in local and foreign trade journals, large litters are not rare at all. The upper limit seems to be seven young per litter; however, this is not at all desirable since such young are frequently too weak to survive. Females with larger litters are often physically drained of energy from nursing all these young and require longer periods to regain good condition. Therefore, under such circumstances it is indeed advisable to remove some of the young from such females and place them, if possible, with other females nursing fewer young. Alternatively, these young can also be raised by bottle-feeding, which is very labor-intensive and requires much time; moreover, success in rearing the young to the weaning stage is not always assured.

The answer to the recurring question of whether the progeny of chinchillas contains more males or females is inconclusive. As a guideline, large breeding facilities produce on the average 55 to 60% bucks and 40 to 45%

females. The actual sex ratio varies within these ranges from one year to the next.

One normally assumes a base line of 100% for reproduction in chinchilla breeding. Since fertility can be affected by many outside influences, the actual reproductive rate can vary widely. With a gestation period of 111 days it is generally expected that a female will produce five litters in two years. Initially these consist of one to two young, later increasing to up to four young. A practical example can be taken from the results of a North American facility with a production average of 4.8 young per female per year; 107 females gave birth to 518 young. This included 10 females that did not produce any litters.

Systematics of Chinchillas (Chinchillidae)
by Dr. Th. Haltenorth, Munich

Chinchillas form — within the rodents or Rodentia, the largest of all mammalian orders — their own family, Chinchillidae, which is phylogenetically closest to the guinea pigs (Caviidae), agoutis (Dasyproctidae), pacaranas (Dinomyidae), capybaras, water hogs, and carpinchos (Hydrochoeridae), and coypus or nutria (Capromyidae). They are of guinea pig to rabbit size and have medium-size, roundish ears, a bushy tail of about half the body length, and a dense light to dark gray coat.

Chinchillas as a family are colonial animals that live in rocky crevices or burrows and are mainly crepuscular or diurnal in their activity patterns. The natural range of these animals is essentially the west and south of South America, from Peru, Bolivia, and northern Argentina southward. Three genera are recognized.

The largest chinchilla is the Plains Viscacha, genus *Lagostomus*, with one species, *L. maximus*. It occupies the pampas from Buenos Aires to Patagonia. The body length of this species is about 50 cm, tail length about 18 cm. The three-toed hind legs of this species are twice as long as the four-toed front legs. It forms colonies containing 20 to 50 animals that dig extensive branching burrows, where once a year the females give birth to a litter of two or three young. The young are essentially precocious, with a fur coat and open eyes, and are quite capable of running about. The Plains Viscacha, *Lagostomus maximus* (Desmarest, 1820), occurs as four subspecies in Patagonia and central Argentina, from Buenos Aires to Mendoza and up to the Gran Chaco, as well as at Cuzco (Santa Ana), central Peru, as has been reported.

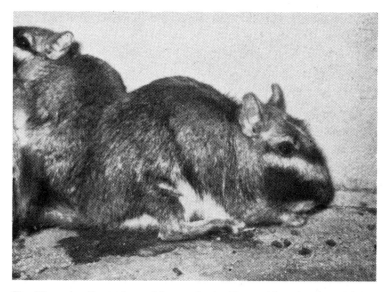

The Viscacha (*Lagostomus*) is a rodent with worthless fur that also belongs to the family Chinchillidae. Viscachas live in colonies and dig burrows that are extensively branched. They are found in the Argentinian Pampas to Patagonia.

Considerably smaller viscachas belong to the genus *Lagidium*, the Mountain Viscachas or Peruvian Hares. Two species inhabit the mountains and high plateaus of Peru, Bolivia, Chile to the Strait of Magellan, and western Argentina. Their body length is about 30-45 cm, tail length about 20-40 cm. The most northern species is *L. peruanum* (Meyen, 1833), with four subspecies occurring in Peru. Geographically the southern species is *L. viscacia* (Molina, 1782), with 12 subspecies distributed in Bolivia and western northern, central, and southern Argentina, as well as in the border region between Chile and Argentina to 50 degrees latitude south. In this genus the ears are very large and upright, leading to the name "Peruvian Hares." The tail is over half to almost as long as the body, however.

The smallest species of the family are the True Chinchillas, *Chinchilla*, with two species in Peru, Bolivia, Chile, and western Argentina. The Short-tailed Chinchilla, *Chinchilla chinchilla* (Lichtenstein, 1829)* is characterized by its relatively short tail (compared with body length) and by its shorter, rounder ears. The natural range of this species is the western slopes of the coastal Cordilleras, between 9 degrees and 23 degrees latitude south, mainly in Peru as well as west-southwestward into the Bolivian and western Argentine Andes (Province Potosi in Bolivia up to Province La Rioja in western Argentina). This species is divided into two subspecies.

The second species is the Long-tailed Chinchilla, *Chinchilla lanigera* (Molina, 1782). It occurs in the coastal highlands and valleys in the interior of Chile between 25 degrees and 32 degrees latitude south. *C. lanigera* has a relatively longer tail and longer ears, but the body length is smaller. It apparently has not developed any subspecies, but color variations of the pelage are also substantial in this species. This species is the one usually raised for fur, and unless otherwise stated is the one meant by the general name chinchilla in this book; it will also be called Velligera and Lanigera. Because of substantial confusion about the popular, trade, and scientific names of these animals, the classification followed here is listed below in some detail.

*American Editor's Comment:
From the synonymy presented later, it appears that the specific name *chinchilla* Lichtenstein, 1829, is preoccupied by *chinchilla* Fischer, 1814, a synonym of *C. lanigera*. If this is correct, then the short-tailed Chinchilla would have to take the next available name, *brevicaudata* Waterhouse; 1848, which in fact is the name normally used in American and English scientific literature. To avoid confusing an already confused situation even more, we have adhered to the German usage in this volume.

Chinchillas, *Chinchilla* Bennett, 1829

1) Short-tailed Chinchilla, *Chinchilla chinchilla* (Lichtenstein, 1829)

- *Distinguishing characteristics:* Body relatively large (body length 30-38 cm); tail and ears rather short relative to body; ears roundish.
- *Distribution:* Western slopes of the coastal Cordilleras in Peru and northern Chile, between 9 degrees and 23 degrees latitude south, also westward and southward in Bolivian and western Argentinian Andes from the Province Potosi in Bolivia to the Province La Rioja in western Argentina.

A) Greater Short-tailed Chinchilla, *Chinchilla chinchilla chinchilla* (Lichtenstein, 1829)

- *Other names:* True, Precious, Royal, or Peruvian Chinchilla, La Chinchilla Real, La Chinchilla Indiana.
- *Synonymy: Eriomys chinchilla* Lichtenstein, 1829.
  Lagostomus laniger Wagler, 1831.
  Chinchilla brevicaudata Waterhouse, 1848.
  Chinchilla brevicaudata variety *major* Burmeister, 1879.
- *Distinguishing characteristics:* Body length 36-38 cm; tail length, including distal hairs, 14-16 cm; ear length 4-5 cm; ears roundish. This subspecies has the shortest ears and tail relative to the body length.
- *Duration of gestation period:* Unknown.
- *Longevity:* Presumably up to 22 years. No further details are known.
- *Distribution:* Western coastal Cordilleras in Peru and northern Chile, between 9 degrees and 23 degrees latitude south, at elevations from 3,000 m to 6,000 m and higher.
- *Population status:* Has probably already been extinct for several decades in its natural range and has never been maintained in domesticated form. This subspe-

cies had the most valuable pelt.

B) Lesser Short-tailed Chinchilla, *Chinchilla chinchilla boliviana* Brass, 1911

- *Other names:* Mountain, Bolivian, La Plata, Argentine, or Cordilleras Chinchilla, La Chinchilla Cordillerana, La Chinchilla del Altiplano, La Chinchilla Boliviana, La Chinchilla de la Plata, Boliviano, Brevicaudata.
- *Synonymy: Chinchilla boliviana* Brass, 1911.
  Chinchilla intermedia Dennler, 1939.
  "Brevicaudata" of fur breeders.
- *Distinguishing characteristics:* Body length 30-32 cm; tail length, including distal hairs 14-16 cm; ear length 4-5 cm; ears roundish.
- *Duration of gestation period:* 120-128 days.
- *Litters:* On the average two litters per year, rarely three, with one to four young; mean number of young per year is 4.2.
- *Longevity:* 22 years.
- *Distribution:* Bolivian and western Argentine Andes from the Province Potosi in Bolivia to the Province La Rioja in western Argentina. Occurs at elevations from 2,500 to 4,000 m.
- *Population status:* Extinct over wide areas of its range. Has recently been protected by legislation so that it is hoped that this subspecies can also be maintained in its natural habitat. Less common now as domesticated form.

2) Long-tailed Chinchilla, *Chinchilla lanigera* (Molina, 1782)

- *Other names:* Coastal, Lesser, Hybrid, or Chilena Chinchilla, La Chinchilla Costina, La Chinchilla Chilena, La Chinchilla Bastarda, Lanigera, Velligera.

- *Synonymy: Mus laniger* Molina, 1782.

    Cricetus chinchilla Fischer, 1814.

    Chinchilla velligera Prell, 1934.

    Lommus lanigera Tiedemann, 1803.

    Cricetus lanigera Desmarest, 1822.

    "Velligera" of fur breeders.
- *Distinguishing characteristics:* Body length 25-26 cm; tail length, including distal hairs, 17-18 cm; ear length 6 cm; ears relatively elongated.
- *Duration of gestation period:* 108-111 days.
- *Litters:* On the average two per year, frequently also three, with one to six young each: mean number per year 4.8.
- *Longevity:* About 18 years.
- *Distribution:* Coastal cordilleras, including highlands and interior valleys in Chile between 25 degrees and 32 degrees latitude south, at elevations up to 3,000 m.
- *Population status:* Largely extinct over natural range. Recently protected by legislation, so it is hoped some populations will survive in the wild. Most common domesticated form.

Apart from the Chinchilla species, the Mountain Viscacha or Peruvian Hare, *Lagidium,* has also been of interest to the fur trade. The pelt of these animals is also rather dense, but it is not as woolly, of brownish coloration, and nearly as fine as that of the true Chinchillas. The trade refers to these pelts as "Chinchillones," that is, Large Chinchillas, but they are not highly valued. According to Brehm, only a few hundred were shipped each year to Europe toward the end of the 19th Century.

The pelt of the Plains Viscacha (*Lagostomus*) is of very little value since it is rather coarse and not very dense. The meat of these animals is keenly sought after by native Indians as a delicacy. Farmers, on the other hand, hunt them because their widely branching burrows tend

A normal standard gray chinchilla is the most common type of chinchilla that is raised on chinchilla farms. Odd colored chinchillas are of little value to a commercial furrier.

Lagidium peruanum, Peruvian Hare. From *Welt und Haus,*1858.

Peruvian Hare

Cuvierian Hare

Wooly Hare   Buenos Aires Hare   Chinchilla

Chinchillas and their relatives. From a lithograph, about 1850, of unknown source.

to cause farm animals to break through and break their legs. They have been persecuted nearly to extinction.

As substitutes for genuine chinchilla pelts the fur trade used to utilize the Chinchilla Rats or Comb Rats. They come from western South America, where they are called Tucu-tucos, Tocoros, or Tojos. The scientific name is *Ctenomys*, family Ctenomyidae. These animals look like gophers and live in burrows. Today they are rarely available commercially. Their pelts are very loose and usually yellowish, and even the best of them could never even remotely resemble a good chinchilla pelt.

Left: Long distance view of a housing unit of a present-day chinchilla farm. *Right:* Close view of the lower row of cages and the automatic watering system.

The tools and equipment necessary for maintaining an efficient watering system should always be on hand for needed repairs.

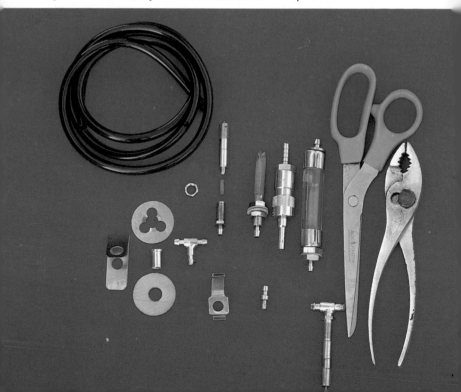

Cages not serviced by an automatic watering system are provided with individual water bottles. This chinchilla is lapping water from a glass spout. The water bottle in the adjacent cage has a metal spout.

A History of
Chinchilla Breeding

The first one to think of breeding chinchillas for profit must have been the Jesuit priest Juan Ignazio Molina (born on 24 June 1740 in Talca, Chile; died 12 September 1829 in Bologna). He was librarian for the Society of Jesus, and his legacy was the publication *Saggio sulla storia naturale del Chile (An Attempt at a Natural History of Chile)*. This book originally was published in Italian in Bologna in 1782. A German translation appeared in 1786. I have here in front of me a copy of the second edition (also published in Bologna, in 1810), where it says on page 249, literally translated:

"....2. The chinchilla......is a type of field mouse, which is eagerly sought after because of the fine fur (coat) it is covered with. It can thus be described as a woolly fur which is as silky soft, as if spun by garden spiders. It is of an ash-gray color and sufficiently long for spinning....5 or 6 young are born twice a year, and it is so tame and of such tractable manner that it can be picked up and it neither bites nor does it make any attempts to flee... as such it is extremely clean and one does not have to be concerned that ones clothes become soiled or that they give off a bad odor; in fact, they are free of any such odor as is associated with the other mice (species); therefore they can be bred in homes at very low costs largely compensated for by the wool....the old Peruvians, who worked much harder than those of today, used to make bed spreads and other valuable garments out of chinchilla wool...."

With these words Molina provided not only a rather accurate description — presumably based on his own observations — but he can also be considered as the originator of breeding chinchillas for profit. But it must be emphasized at this point that he did not intend to breed them for their pelts but solely for their "very fine wool." Presumably he had actually seen such garments made during the Inca period, which gave him the idea to breed chinchillas. In fact, this idea has been resurrected again more recently. The hair used for spinning purposes apparently comes from unsalable pelts that can not be used by the fur trade, because a large number do not conform to the standards and requirements of the pelt industry. So far there is virtually no other usage for pelts that are below quality standards or that are damaged.

The first literature reference to chinchillas dates back to 1591 in a book published in Seville, entitled *Historia Natural y Moral de los Indios*, written by Father Joseph de Acosta (1540-1599), also a Jesuit. A verbatim quote of the old Spanish text follows:

"About mountain animals. Chinchillas are another type of small animals such as squirrels. They have a fur (coat) that is of wonderful softness. Their furs are worn for decorative purposes and for health reasons, in order to protect the stomach and other parts, which require moderate warmth. There are also blankets or bed spreads made of chinchilla hair. They occur in the mountain chain of Peru...".

Another relevant literature contribution comes from Clarke (1961). He cites a report by the English seafarer Sir John Hawkins (1532-1595), where it says: "Among other things they have small animals which look like squirrels but they are grey; the fur (coat) is the finest, softest and most remarkable I have ever seen; it is highly valued (for obvious reasons) in Peru. Few of these pelts ever reach Spain because they are difficult to obtain; they call this animal chinchilla and there are large numbers of them."

This cage designed to house a single pet chinchilla has a metal sand bath box that can be pulled out for disposal and replacement of used sand. The cage can also be lifted for removal of soiled litter on the tray underneath.

A chinchilla in the act of shaking the sand off its body. Instead of placing the sand in a box, it is simply spread over a board in this case.

A food hopper is very convenient in feeding a big stock of chinchillas. It is not necessary to open the cage's door to deliver the daily ration or to collect leftovor food.

Juan Ignacio Molina (1740-1829), author of the idea of breeding chinchillas.

Although it can be assumed that Molina was aware of Acosta's report that appeared 219 years before his own book was published, it is conspicuous that even this early report may have referred to clothing made from the hair of chinchillas. Regrettably, all my own attempts to secure further details about this from museums, archeologists, and textile experts have been futile.

Apparently chinchillas had been kept as domestic animals and pets by the old Peruvians and the Incas. This may have also been true of other South American Indians living in the areas occupied by chinchillas.

There were repeated early attempts to breed these animals in captivity. The first one I know of was made by the naturalist Sir John Murray (born in Coburg, Ontario, on 3 March 1841: died Kirliston, Scotland, on 16 March 1914). Apparently his efforts were made on a large scale. Murray was a member of the famous Challenger Expedition from 1882 to 1895. The results of this expedition were published in numerous folio volumes. Sir John Murray is alleged to have had an area in Vallenar, Chile, fenced in and to have released chinchillas there in 1874. Presumably this involved several hundred animals, but they were all killed by predators. Anyway, this is the way it was reported by an old Indian who claimed to have been a witness and who was later employed by the chinchilla breeder Martin Nilsson on his farm in Argentina.

The first reliable report of a successful breeding attempt in captivity comes from Frederico Albert (1900), who was director of the zoological and botanical research station (Ministry for Industry and Employment) at Santiago, Chile, at the turn of the century. He reports in his first article on the subject of chinchillas, "La Chinchilla," about a certain Francisco Irrazaval in Santiago, who had received a pair of chinchillas (presumably Lanigera) from the Province of Coquimbo in 1895. "The food preferred (by these animals) was lucerne clover, damp (?!) lettuce and dry bread. The first chinchilla was born that same year, on 16 October 1895. It had a total length (tip of snout to base of tail) of 6.5 to 7 cm, a complete fur coat and was able to run from the first day onward. Irrazaval exhibited his chinchilla family at the National Agricultural Show. He was awarded a silver medal for the young chinchilla as a first prize and a copper medal (second prize) for the parent pair." Albert further reports that in the time thereafter the pair continued to produce two litters a year, as is

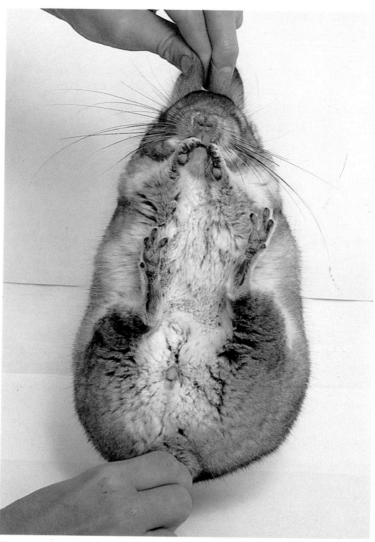

The correct way of holding the ears and the tail prior to lifting a chinchilla. Both ears must be held at the same time and the tail grasped close to the body.

Facing page: Always hold your pet chinchilla with two hands; one hand always supporting the rear end and the other, around the body proper. A frightened pet will react by shedding its fur.

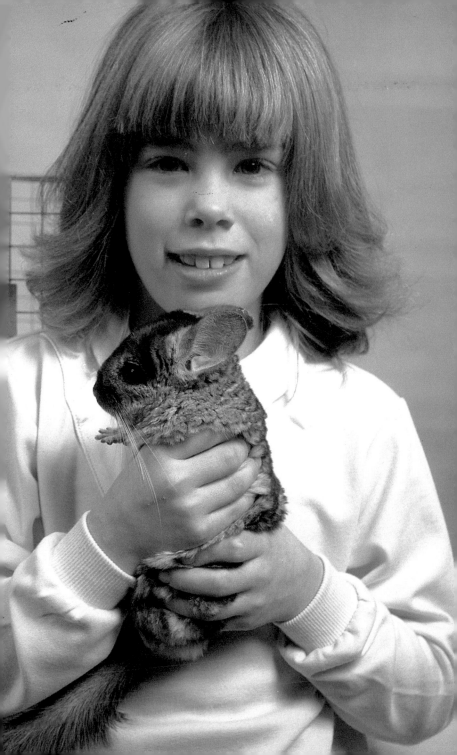

The first illustration of a chinchilla, a colored lithograph (1830) from H. Lichtenstein. Illustration of a new or little known rodent.

common among rodents. The first litter was dropped in October, the second one in March; each contained two young. The captive-born young, in turn, bred about a year later. Unfortunately, the outbreak of an epidemic during the summer of 1898 ruined this excellent breeding success, and all the animals, 13 at that time, died within a period of two months.

The London Zoological Garden received the first live chinchilla as early as 1829. Bennet observed this animal at great length and provided a detailed description. Comments from Prof. Dr. Pechuel-Loesche, editor of the mammal section of the 1893 edition of Brehm's *Tierleben*, about this event are as follows: "Whether this animal drinks is questionable: it appears that it can do without any (supplementary) drinking liquid. This species, which has been kept regularly at the London Zoo and where it has repeatedly been bred, appears more suitable than any other rodent for domestication."

At the turn of the century there was an abundant offering of wild-caught chinchilla pelts so nobody worried much about the possible extermination of these animals due to excessive hunting pressure. Frederico Albert's call for the protection of chinchillas and his recommendations for a management program were efforts made in vain, just as were the export restrictions for pelts at the beginning of this century. When the governments of Bolivia, Chile, Argentina, and Peru finally prohibited the hunting and collecting of chinchillas and the trade in their pelts, it was already too late. Only the fact that these animals had been virtually exterminated until it had become uneconomical to hunt them may have saved the last remnants of these animals in the wild. With permission from the Argentine government in 1927, Martin Nilsson established a breeding farm for Brevicaudata near Abra Pampa, Province Jujuy. This facility was later taken over by the State. There are several breeding farms in South America, including some with a few hundred animals, but there are no further details available. One of these, the Criadero de Chinchillas S.A., is a public corporation and is located in San Roque, Santiago de Chile, at an elevation of 3,300 m.

No history of chinchilla breeding would be complete without mentioning the buck Hans, kept by the Leipzig furrier Richard Gloeck (1862-1946), also known as the "Chinchilla King." He had acquired this animal at an age of about two years from an Italian family in La Serena, Chile. The Italians owned three good-quality animals, and parted reluctantly from the buck only after money had changed hands and some persuasive words were spoken. Mr. Gloeck and wife took Hans, as they

Above: A housing setup for a single pet chinchilla should include a wire cage, a heavy ceramic feeding dish, a water bottle, and a layer of litter material underneath. A cardboard box will be inevitably chewed and should not be included. *Left:* Pine shavings are marketed for the bedding of small mammals and packaged in a variety of sizes. Heavily scented wood like cedar is not recommended.

Right: Guinea pig pellets have been found to be a good substitute for chinchilla pellets. However, try to get chinchilla pellets that are specially formulated for the chinchilla's food requirements. *Below:* Alfalfa (lucerne) is sold either as loose or cubed form. Your chinchilla must have good hay for normal development.

Richard Gloeck,
at one time the
"Chinchilla King"
of Leipzig.

called the animal, on a long and arduous journey. This is only of interest because it shows that chinchillas are really tougher than is generally assumed. They went from La Serena by boat to Coquimbo, from there to Mollendo, Peru, and onward by train to Arequipa, Peru, the capital of the administrative district of the same name. This town is located at an elevation of 2,329 m, and in order to get to it a mountain of 4,430 m elevation had to be crossed. In order to adjust to the high altitude air the party made a rest stop of a few days. From there the journey continued with a 12-hour steamer trip across Lake Titicaca, which is located at an elevation of 3,812 m, and onward to the Bolivian capital La Paz, 3,600 m to 3,800 m elevation, for a one-week stop-over. The next leg of the trip commenced with an eight-day trip down to the coast at Callao, the port of Lima, then on to Panama. Since at that time the Panama Canal was still under construction, they crossed the isthmus by land. Along the equator it was very hot and the rainy season produced continuous downpours. Since they missed their connection in Jamaica, the couple and Hans had to wait for a week for the next boat at a time when it was extremely hot. Next they took a boat to New York where the temperature was -8°C in the middle of December. When the boat crossed the Gulf Stream on the way to Europe it got temporarily warmer, but when they finally arrived in Hamburg (in 1912) and continued their journey to Leipzig the temperature was -11°C. In spite of all this, Hans, who had been accommodated in a wire cage, arrived in good condition. This motivated Mr. Gloeck to arrange for the acquisition of a female through a contact in South America. This animal made a sea journey along the west coast of South America through the Strait of Magellan and also arrived safely in Leipzig.

The first encounter between the two animals led to a severe fight. Later they adjusted to each other and there was indeed hope for progeny, but the female suddenly died. This could have been the beginning of chinchilla breeding in Europe, and Mr. Gloeck had already recognized at that time the potentials of such a venture. Hans lived until 1923 and gave much viewing pleasure to Mr. Gloeck's business visitors, particularly when he took the animal out of its cage. The diet of this animal consisted of green food, fruit, and apple peels, which were given daily. I was assured that during its 11-year tenure in Leipzig the animal was never given any water. Until the

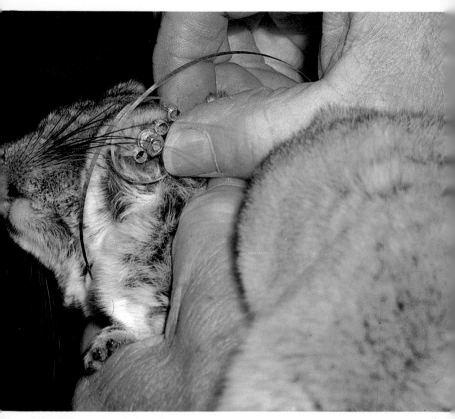

A breeding collar is installed around the neck of a female chinchilla to prevent her from entering an opening that is intended exclusively for the passage of a male into the mating cage.

Facing page: Suggested equipment for maintaining a pet chinchilla should consist of brushes of various sizes, a water bottle with metal spout and holder, a dish for special treats, a hay rack, and a food hopper.

very end its fur was in excellent condition. As an additional point, it should be mentioned here that Chapman had a chinchilla (the eighth one that was collected for him in the wild) that he named "Old Hoff" that reached an age of 22 years.

A Mrs. Johnstone from Tonbridge, Kent, England, received a dozen Laniger pairs in 1911 or 1912. This lady was a well-known collector and breeder of exotic birds. These activities may have given her the idea to make the first serious attempt in Europe to breed chinchillas. She soon recognized that the animals — apparently kept out in the open — did not do well in the damp English air, so she then decided to house some of the animals in 3 x 1.5 m huts and some in colonial enclosures of 3.6 x 3.6 m; the bottom was covered with sand. The colonial enclosures also contained sandstone tiles that hid the nest boxes. Following this move the animals started to breed quite well until eventually there were 40 to 50 animals. They were given a random diet of carrots, peanuts, lucerne, and green food until the owner had a better idea of the specific dietary requirements of her animals. Unfortunately, the start of World War I forced Mrs. Johnstone to surrender her chinchillas and her valuable Mikado pheasant collection to various large zoos. There the animals died, apparently because of the incorrect care they were given.

It was not until much later, in 1938, that chinchillas again bred in England. A certain Roberts from Eastbourne made another attempt and imported a few pairs of chinchillas from South America. Obviously these animals were given the right kind of care since one pair is alleged to have produced not less than 16 young within a span of 14 months. Unfortunately, I do not know anything about the fate of this facility.

During the same year Hans died (on 23 February 1923), the American Mathias F. Chapman brought to

Inglewood, California, 11 *Chinchilla lanigera* that had been caught by Indians in the Andes. These were eight bucks and three females that were brought under considerable protective measures over the equator. Chapman had been a manager for the American Anaconda Copper Company in Chile for many years in some of the copper mines located 3,000 m high in the Andes in northern Chile. A local blacksmith showed him, quite by accident, some chinchilla pelts that he had received from an old Indian. The beauty of these pelts made such an impression on Chapman that he asked this man to catch him some live chinchillas, since he always enjoyed watching them. Eventually he had 23 Indian trappers working for him. One of the captured animals, a buck that he named Duque de Tucuman (Duke of Tucuman) had endured an 11-day journey in a gasoline can strapped to a horse's saddle without water and food before Chapman got him. Chapman's first reaction was to feed and water the poor animal, but the Indian said that this would kill the animal and he wanted his money up front. Once again, this report indicates that chinchillas are extremely durable and tough, and the Indian clearly knew that these animals do not drink in the wild. This animal was about two years old when Chapman received it, and it lived for about another 18 years.

Chapman had recognized the enormous potential of breeding chinchillas in captivity, so he decided, when his contract terminated in 1922, to take up chinchilla breeding. Since hunting chinchillas or even the possession of their pelts was already prohibited by law, he had great difficulties in obtaining the necessary export permit. He was given an export license for only 11 of the 17 animals he owned. He selected the most attractive and strongest animals, the previously mentioned eight bucks and three females (other sources list these as seven males and four females). In any event, they were all

On a chinchilla farm hay is never in short supply. It is never stored for long periods because moldy hay can destroy a stock of chinchillas that are sensitive to fungal infection.

A chinchilla nibbling a twig of hay it pulled from above the cage. Hay if placed directly on the cage's floor will get trampled and soiled within a short time.

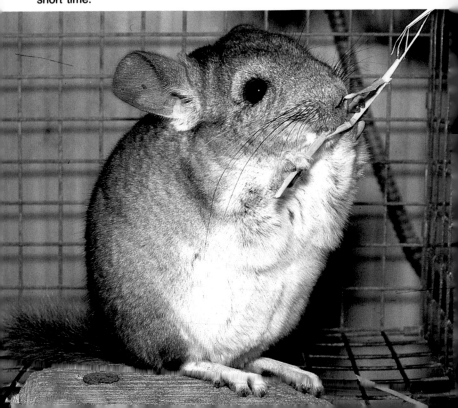

Watch closely the effect of whatever greens you offer your pet chinchilla. If abnormal droppings are produced, refrain from giving that particular green food again.

Chinchilla lanigera. According to an American report all the animals had dropped their hair by arrival in San Pedro, California, (due to the heat of the equator crossing) but it grew in again in due course. One animal died during transport and one young was born. After overcoming numerous obstacles and setbacks, Chapman's stock grew to about 100 animals.

Then 35 animals were stolen from his facility in Inglewood, California, and shipped to Europe (at least according to an American source). Whether these stolen animals died due to insufficient care and maintenance or for other reasons remains unanswered. The fact, however, is that the new "owner" had little joy with these animals; they died one by one, thus turning a less noteworthy page in the annals of chinchilla breeding. Chapman made every attempt to recover the stolen animals once he knew of their whereabouts, but it was too late. Only five animals were still alive by the time the court had decided in his favor.

Later he moved some of his breeding activities to Tehachapi, California, and he sold breeding stock from both of his farms, which brought him substantial returns. Regrettably, Chapman was able to follow the further development in this new industry only until 1934. He died on 12 December 1934, at an age of only 52 years, without ever becoming part of the worldwide spread of chinchilla breeding of which he was the originator. His son, Donald F. Chapman, took over breeding. He sold the farm to the animal dealer Willis D. Parker in July, 1955, but he continues to work there as well as run his own operation, and he intends to eventually bring his farm at Inglewood up to an annual harvest of 1000 skins as well as supplying quality stud bucks.

The sensational spread of chinchilla breeding in the United States and Canada is exclusively due to the foresight and endurance of Mathias F. Chapman, for chinchilla breeding in Canada owes its existence also to Chapman. A Canadian who had recognized the commercial potential of breeding chinchillas brought the first animals to the Province of Alberta in 1937. From there chinchilla breeding spread rapidly throughout Canada. Exactly 10 years later the Canadian chinchilla breeders organized themselves and formed the National Chinchilla Breeders of Canada.

The sale of pelts takes place via the New York Auction Company and the Mechutan Fur Corporation, which both receive an equal share. Part of the pelts is sold directly to furriers for manufacture into garments.

The former offered its pelts in top quality under the famous brand name "Aurora"; the Empress Chinchilla Alliance (ECA) sells under the name "Empress." The latter used to have an agency in Glostrup, Denmark. In Europe, the Chinchilla Pelt Center Schreiber & Co. Munich, recently has come into the scene, as well as the Trade Association of German Fur Breeders (WDP), Frankfurt a. Main, both accepting chinchilla pelts for preparation and sale.

In countries with winter temperatures below zero it is generally customary to maintain the breeding stock in enclosed rooms that are heated to at least 15°C in order to prevent the drinking water from freezing over. According to reports in trade journals, during the early years of chinchilla breeding in Canada as well as the United States, the breeding enclosures were set up outdoors. A protective roof provided cover against snow, rain, and excessive sun. European breeders have repeatedly made similar attempts with outdoor enclosures, but the results were apparently not satisfactory. One reason that speaks against using this type of housing is the danger of the animals catching a cold; they are also essentially unprotected against theft. Therefore, it is now common practice to keep chinchillas in enclosed facili-

Appearance of abnormal chinchilla droppings. Droppings that are too wet, too dry, and shrunken are possible signs of the existence of an intestinal problem.

Normal chinchilla droppings should be plump, moist, and shiny.

It is easy to recognize incisors with abnormal growth. They are not straight, slanting instead, and do not meet each other squarely.

These normal incisors are straight, with smooth cutting edge and yellow color. Newly born chinchillas have white teeth that turn later into the normal yellow color.

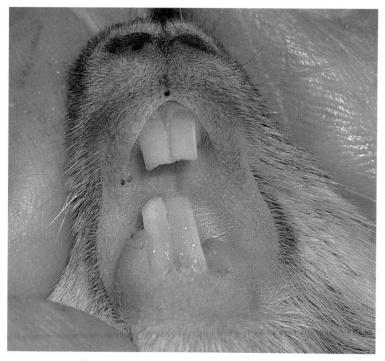

ties. Unfortunately, there are many breeding farms that do not deserve this name because the animals are accommodated under very poor conditions with insufficient fresh air and light. Moreover, the breeding rooms are often damp, which is totally incompatible with the requirements of these animals from desert-like habitats. Consequently it is not surprising when the breeding results are correspondingly poor, especially when the animals are not kept under proper hygienic conditions.

Following Chapman's efforts, the next breeding attempt was made by the engineer Frederik Holst in Norway in 1934. He brought 16 Brevicaudata from Buenos Aires to Paris and from there to Oslo so that he could house the animals on his farm, Gisle, County Asker, southwest of the capital. They arrived at their destination on 20 August 1934. Shortly before that, 11 members from an English company were given a collecting permit by the government of Bolivia for a high fee. This hunting party was less successful than Holst and had to return empty handed. The company was dissolved with heavy losses to all partners involved in this venture. According to a Norwegian source, Holst got his 16 animals from a South American woman who operated a breeding facility near Buenos Aires. Although Holst must have known the habitat conditions of chinchillas since he had lived in the Andes for some time with his family, his chinchilla breeding facility, established at considerable cost, did not succeed. After some initial successes his animals as well as those of some other owners started to die. By 1937, a total of only 31 animals was left in three breeding farms.

Since then interest in chinchillas and the number of chinchillas kept have grown considerably in Norway, where the breeding of silver foxes had also gotten its start. There now are a large number of chinchilla breeding farms in Norway and there is also a breeders' association. Breeders in many other countries have also formed associations.

Most of the European chinchilla breeding facilities are in West Germany, the Soviet Union, and Denmark. There is also a large number of them in Sweden, as well as some in Holland and in France. Beyond that, there are also chinchilla farms in Switzerland, Italy, and Greece. Finally, it must be mentioned that chinchillas are also being bred in Poland, East Germany, and in other Eastern Bloc countries.

In West Germany chinchilla breeding was started in Stuttgart-Hohenheim by the now deceased Albert Muenzing. He acquired a few Lanigera pairs in the spring of 1953.

The size of captive chinchilla populations in different countries can only be estimated as official figures are not available. Records from the various associations also do not mean very much because membership numbers and breeding stock levels keep changing and many breeders do not belong to a professional association. The number of animals actually being kept will become clearer when the economic basis of chinchilla breeding is shifted from the sale and trade of live animals toward harvesting skins.

It is interesting to speculate how chinchilla breeding throughout the world might develop in the future. In contrast to the production of other fur-bearing animals, chinchilla breeding has taken a totally different pathway, and that is expected to continue. When silver fox breeding started in the United States in 1867, nobody suspected the enormous development that occurred. This reached its peak in 1939 with 1.2 million skins as its highest worldwide level, but now it has declined to an insignificant number. It has long since been overtaken by mink breeding, not only in the "traditional" fur-farming countries such as the United States, Can-

This mosaic chinchilla obviously has inherited some of the markings and color of standard gray chinchilla and white chinchilla ancestors.

A beige chinchilla is a light-colored individual with red eyes.

ada, and Norway, but also in many Eastern Bloc countries where mink pelts have become a significant source of hard foreign currencies. How large the breeding populations of mink are can hardly be estimated, but if one assumes an annual skin harvest of 15 million worldwide, then there is presumably a breeding population of some 5 million minks of all color types.

Chinchilla pelts and fur garments made of them had been practically forgotten by the time commercial chinchilla breeding started. Therefore, it required considerable determined public relations efforts to convince the public, and women in particular, of the unique beauty of chinchilla furs. For that purpose the American breeder associations have spent large amounts of money in order to generate a market for their product. They modeled their campaign after the PR (public relations) and advertising campaigns by the American breeders of mutation minks. To this day they still have sizable advertising budgets because it is not enough to create an interest in a product — the secret of effective publicity is to constantly remind the public of it.

In some respects the situation for the sale of chinchilla pelts is unusual because chinchilla furs, shawls, jackets, and coats are not utility or street furs made for hard wear. Instead, these garments are always limited to a selected few, just as diamonds and emeralds, sapphires, and other precious stones always remain a luxury not affordable by the vast majority of people. It is estimated that there is a world production of up to 150,000 skins per year, but of these only a very small portion falls into the top quality category. With mink pelts this is estimated to be about 10% of total production; it can be assumed that this also applies to chinchillas.

Care and Maintenance

Since chinchillas are crepuscular and nocturnal animals, it was initially assumed that they could be kept without difficulties in basements and cellars or dark garages. Unfortunately this belief still persists occasionally today in some quarters, generally in order to facilitate the sale of breeding stock. However, it has now been shown that chinchillas also require some sunlight. Moreover, they like to catch a few warming rays of sunshine in the late afternoon just before the sun sets whenever they have the opportunity. Apart from the fact that these animals do not survive for long in damp cellar air, they should be given quarters in a bright and preferably dry room. If such a room is available it must also be sufficiently large for a number of chinchilla cages so that a proper start for the colony is guaranteed. However, if the breeding activities are later expanded to set up for commercial pelt production, a more sizable structure (a shed or a brick structure) will be required. Few breeders will be in the same lucky position as chinchilla breeders in sunny California who also use sheds, but with the enclosures located along the outside walls so that the animals are living partially outdoors.

Due to frequent precipitation in our German climate, there is really no other alternative but to maintain chinchillas in enclosed, draft-protected rooms. It must always be kept in mind that chinchillas are very sensitive to drafts, particularly when planning the ventilation. These rooms should also be as bright as possible.

In order to accommodate as many breeding animals as possible in a single room, the next step is to stack the cages one on top of the other. Whether this is done on wall-mounted brackets or free-standing wooden or metal shelving (so that several rows can be placed above each other) is up to the individual breeder, his operational requirements, and, of course, his financial resources.

Anyone handy with tools can save much money by making his own cages and enclosures. Wooden cages have the disadvantage that the animals frequently tend to chew on them. The wire panels should be secured with metal staples along the inside of the cage frame to keep the animals away from the wood as much as possible. The use of square or hexagonal wire mesh, either hand-woven or machine manufactured hardware cloth, is also dependent upon available finances. The cheapest method is to use galvanized small-gauge chicken wire for the top and sides. It is important to make sure that there are no wire ends protruding into the cage to inflict injuries on the animals. Point-welded wire mesh is now the most commonly used material because it is more rigid and does not require any support structure. The newest material now used is stainless steel mesh.

Because of modern assembly line manufacturing methods, practical and easily cleanable enclosures and cages for chinchillas are now available at moderate costs. Advertisements from manufacturers appear in all appropriate journals, but it is advisable to purchase these cages locally if possible in order to avoid delays and additional transport costs, especially since several such cages usually are required to eventually enlarge the breeding facility. Wooden cages are no longer used. Since enclosures and cages are permanently roofed over they will last for many years.

Enclosures made of iron (angle iron or metal rods) are far more hygienic and will last practically forever, but they are also much more costly and require more specialized tools and mechanical aptitude for their construction if they are to be homemade.

In any event, the animals must be given sufficient room to move about and be able to stay out of each other's way, otherwise there may be problems. Some years ago the preferred cage size was from 40-70 x 80 x 60 cm, but now that mostly polygamous breeding is being done, breeders have changed over to a cage size of 50 x 50 x 60 cm. Animals designated for skinning are kept in 40 x 40 x 45 cm cages. The commonly used wire thickness is 1.6 mm. A litter tray is attached below the wire bottom and must be cleaned thoroughly at least once a week. The preferred mesh size is 19 mm x 19 mm. It would indeed be desirable if the industry could agree on a standardization of cage sizes, but this will probably take some time to become reality.

Chinchillas kept in polygamous breeding groups are housed in specially designed enclosures. These consist of four or more subdivisions for the females and a passage (run) attached on either side for the buck. In this case, females are fitted with a neck collar made of plastic. This collar serves to prevent the female from leaving its compartment since the collar has a greater diameter than the entrance hole. The buck, which does not wear a collar, can freely enter and leave each female's compartment. Some breeders remove the neck collar once a female has copulated successfully and is actually pregnant. The entrance hole is then closed off or, alternatively, the female is placed into a special littering cage where it is not disturbed. The neck collar could be a hindrance and prevent the female from taking necessary supportive action during parturition (birth), but it does not impede proper feeding and mobility. Such a collar can be obtained commercially.

Most breeders have now changed over to polygamous breeding of chinchillas in these enclosures, which are used primarily for pelt production and for breeding animals to increase the breeding stock. The enclosures are constructed in such a way that four, five, six, or more females are kept together with a single buck. Each female has its own compartment with a sand bath, and it wears a removable neck collar. The male, on the other hand, can enter the compartment of each female by way of runs from the passage way that connect all the compartments. These polygamous enclosures are based on a construction technique developed over many years. All-in-all it is well thought out, but it does not incorporate all possible advantages. It has happened more than once that a particularly aggressive buck has seriously injured or even killed a female that was unwilling to copulate.

Chinchillas living in the wild usually display a characteristic size difference: the females are distinctly larger and more robust, while the bucks are relatively smaller and more delicate. Over the years this difference has been largely equalized, so that there are today — as a consequence of selective breeding — rather impressive and sizable bucks. Therefore, it is understandable that these large animals are not particularly gentle with a female.

In this context it can not be denied that there are also experienced breeders around who want little or nothing to do with neck collars for their animals. There is indeed much that can be said against using these devices. An American breeder, John D. W. Clarke, for instance, insisted that he preferred primarily pair breeding because he would get a larger average litter size than with polygamous breeding. That is, of course, an opinion that can not be simply overlooked. After all, over the years most breeders have switched from pair breeding to polygamous breeding. The reason for this was that breeders felt they had to feed and look after too many bucks with pair breeding. This can not be denied, but then it is also obvious that neither pair breeding nor polygamous breeding fulfills all expectations. Polygamous breeding is also useful for the purpose of obtaining uniform color tones.

Another question over which there is no consensus among breeders is, should chinchilla nest boxes be placed inside the enclosure or should they be suspended from the walls? Recently there has been a trend away from nest boxes because they are not really necessary, they are expensive to buy, and they make cage cleaning more difficult. In contrast to female rabbits, chinchilla females that are about to give birth do not build a nest. Consequently one can do without a nest box for chinchillas, but it is advisable to place a section of coconut palm mat in one corner just before a female is about ready to drop her litter.

If nest boxes are to be used, the access should be arranged in such a way that the young cannot get out during their first few days. This can be done by attaching a sheet metal strip at right angles to serve as a "deflector" along the inside of the upper edge of the nest box and around the lower margin of the access hole. This prevents the loss of young due to colds and other causes.

Large breeding facilities that are housed in their own building should be equipped with a professionally installed lightning rod, since it has been shown that North American chinchilla breeding farms are hit relatively often by lightning. Presumably this is due to the fact that all those metal enclosures and cages in their totality represent a certain electrical field that "attracts" a lightning strike. In this context a peculiar anomaly must be mentioned here: fire insurance companies generally refuse to lower their premiums for a building equipped with a lightning rod.

Since the cages are placed in several rows above each other, each cage must have its own galvanized litter tray to retain the droppings and spilled food. Pull-out trays are the most convenient ones for cleaning purposes.

Another subject on which breeders are unable to

reach a consensus is that of the cage or enclosure bottom. While some prefer to run their animals on a wire mesh bottom, others are of the opinion that this is too cold during the winter, so they use wood shavings on the cage bottom. It can not be denied that a wire mesh bottom without bedding has the advantage of being easy to keep clean since droppings and urine fall through the wire mesh into the litter tray underneath. This sort of maintenance is relatively hygienic. Of course, the wire bottom has to be removable so that it can be taken out periodically and be thoroughly cleaned. Similarly, bottom trays have to be emptied and cleaned frequently.

A run covered with wood shavings as bedding is, of course, much warmer because it keeps the cold from penetrating from below. Advocates of the use of bedding also insist that they have fewer juvenile mortalities than on wire cage floors. This is probably correct because the animals, especially young, do not catch cold that readily. It is, however, important that the wood shavings are not too damp, as this might lead to fungal growth that could be transmitted to the food and so have an adverse affect on the health of the animals. For instance, hay with fungus is absolute poison for chinchillas.

Wire with a smaller mesh size is more expensive than that with larger mesh. It is, of course, important to select the correct wire mesh size so that young chinchillas can not escape through it or — worse — become entrapped in it. The correct mesh width for cage walls and tops is 19 x 19 mm with 1.6 mm wire thickness. The bottom wire mesh should be 8 mm square.

The Agricultural College in Ultuna, Sweden, has had an experimental breeding station for chinchillas operated by the Swedish Fur-Breeders Association since 1959. There, the director of the station, B. Thelander, has constructed some rather simple but practical and inexpensive cages that can be assembled into polygamous breeding groups. Each group consists of five enclosures together with a passage along the back for the buck to have access to all the females. Usually four of the cages contain a female each, while the fifth one is designated as a resting cage for the buck if he is to be kept out of the female cages. Each cage has its own supply of hay, pellets, and drinking water. The wire used for these cages has a mesh size of 12.7 mm square and a wire width of 1 mm. Each cage is 60 cm long, 40 cm wide, and 40 cm high. Immediately adjacent along the back is the run for the buck along the top, with a sand bath below. The distance between adjacent cages is 4.5 cm; this space is filled with hay so that the animals on either side can remove strands of hay, which keeps them occupied. Since these cages can be arranged in two or more levels above each other, it is advisable to maintain a distance of 10 cm between them. Attached below each enclosure is a tray made of 1.25 mm sheet aluminum that collects left over and spilled food, droppings, and urine. The enclosures are supported by a timber frame made of finished (planed) 3.8 cm x 5 cm timber.

As soon as a certain breeding stock level has been attained, thoughts should be given toward housing those animals designated for skinning. Ideally, they should have their own separate stock room. These animals should be given cages with minimum floor dimensions of about 40 cm x 40 cm, with one animal to a cage. Whether it is really important to keep this room dark is as yet unresolved. Some American breeders are of the opinion that this enhances pelt quality.

Each cage must be equipped with a feed container, which should be made of glazed earthenware. The weight of such a container prevents the animal from turning it over, and it is also easy to clean. This dish is for grain or pelleted food that would otherwise fall through the cage bottom. Containers without a glazed surface are difficult to clean and are therefore unhygienic. Food containers attached inside the front of each cage are also very practical, provided they can be filled from the outside without having to open the cage door. Hay can be placed on the bottom, but I believe it is better to put it in a hay rack, which can be easily made out of galvanized wire and attached to one side of the cage. This method stops the hay from becoming soiled or trampled. It goes without saying that a rack must be placed in such a position that even a young animal can reach the hay without problems and that it can be refilled easily.

Since it can sometimes happen that a *supplementary cage* is required, it is advisable to always have one or more spare cages around of the dimensions 60 cm long x 45 cm wide x 30 cm high. To get older animals that do not know each other to adjust to each other, it is absolutely essential to have *mating cages* available. Usually these are of an all-wire construction (with a door at one side) of the dimensions 45 x 25 x 25 cm. A *weighing cage* is also essential equipment. This is even smaller yet so that it can be placed on scales to monitor the weight of individual animals. This is particularly important for pregnant females to monitor progress of the pregnancy and thus accumulate comparative data.

Instead of mating cages, one can sometimes also use so-called *flight cages*. These can be made in several different shapes. Their purpose is mainly to serve as shelter for a frightened chinchilla. Such a cage can very easily be built at home by anyone handy with metal scissors and a soldering iron. All sharp edges and corners must be avoided so that the animals do not injure themselves. The top side must be firmly attached in order to avoid its being lifted off, which would render a flight cage essentially useless. The same design can also be made out

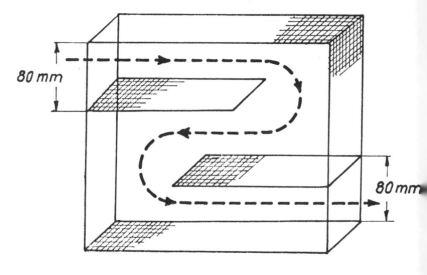

Plan of a flight cage for chinchillas.

of wire mesh of 5 x 5 mm mesh size and fulfill the same purpose. Of even simpler design and construction are flight cages made out of large (1 kilogram) metal cans with the top and bottom neatly cut out so that only a tube remains. This tube is then attached with wire along the middle of one of the cage walls. If an animal is being chased and wants to escape it simply jumps into this tube and is there unreachable for any pursuer because there is only room for one chinchilla inside the tube, a rather clever and simple solution. Common earthenware drainage pipes placed on the bottom of the cage can fulfill the same purpose.

Some chinchillas have the annoying habit of urinating inside the nest box. Since it is impossible to break the animals of this habit, it is suggested that you close off the nest box or remove it completely and put in its place a box without a bottom so that the urine can drain into the bottom tray.

Females that refuse to copulate can drive the inexperienced breeder to distraction. Invariably they viciously attack the buck and so intimidate him that he will make no further attempt. American breeders have come up with a couple of methods designed to prevent injuries. One method utilizes a piece of rubber cut out from a car inner tube. It is 10 cm wide at the bottom, rounded off along the top, and 15 cm high in the middle. A circular hole about 3 to 4 cm in diameter is cut into the upper third of it. This "collar" is pulled over the head of the obstinate female and effectively prevents her from pursuing the male. Once the female has stepped on the piece of rubber with her forefeet and has fallen onto her face a few times, she will become peaceful and will consent — reluctantly — to copulate with the male. Presumably there is no danger from the animal chewing on the rubber. Once this "copulation collar" has served its purpose it should be removed by cautiously cutting it away. This is simpler than trying to pull the piece of rubber back off the head, which is more difficult than putting it on.

Another method to stop biting is by making a sort of muzzle that is pulled over the head and attached around the neck by means of a small belt buckle. It should be made out of soft, thin glove leather, and it must be wide enough so that it can hold the mouth of the animal shut. Using these procedures a difficult pair can be kept together overnight without risking the health and well-being of one of the animals.

The question of providing drinking water is still controversial. European breeders routinely give drinking water to their chinchillas, and this also holds true for most American breeders. But it needs to be mentioned here that there are also experienced breeders who do not provide drinking water for their animals at all, but instead give a daily green food ration as long as seasonally possible. I am also of the opinion that chinchillas *must* have green food but do not necessarily need drinking water. Admittedly, giving green food requires a bit of extra work, especially with large animal holdings, yet cleaning the drinking bottles, which must be kept meticulously clean, also means additional work.

Large farms have changed over to automatic watering systems that are not exactly cheap but in the long run save on labor costs. American breeders are using those automatic watering systems that have been in use for many years on mink farms. They consist of water pipes along the back or front of rows of cages. A separate drinking stem, which is open on top, protrudes obliquely into each cage. These drinking stems are connected to an equalizing container attached to one side. The water level is maintained at equal height in all studs by means of the physical principle of interconnected pipes. This permits the animals to drink whenever they desire.

Another method, but with the same general pipe layout, utilizes pipes with drinking nipples (studs) that point downward into each cage and are closed by a ball valve. Chinchillas and minks quickly learn how to use this system to quench their thirst. When the tongue reaches the ball, water comes out of the valve. The continuous water pressure behind the ball will immediately close the valve again after tongue pressure against the ball has ceased.

The pipes in such automatic water systems are frequently made of plastic. Such a system can readily be taken apart, it does not rust, and it is less expensive to install than metal pipes. However, the actual drinking nipples or studs must be made of metal to stop the animals from chewing on them.

Both systems share the disadvantage of encouraging algal growth that is extremely difficult to remove, especially since there must be no chlorine in drinking water used for chinchillas. Since most municipal water supplies are chlorinated, the drinking water for chinchillas can be passed over an activated carbon filter in order to remove the chlorine. It is assumed that chlorine has an adverse effect on the health of the animals.

Once a day, preferably during the evening feeding, the animals are given their sand (also called dust) bath in a dish. It serves to clean the pelt, and the animals clearly enjoy bathing in it. Anyone seeing the antics of these animals as they rapidly turn in the sand and as each animal waits its turn for the bath to become vacant is usually amazed at this type of behavior commonly associated with birds and poultry.

For the sand bath to be effective the sand must be dust-like, actually a powder. Most suitable for chinchilla sand baths is "Attapulgus" bathing sand. Professional journals also list other types and brands commercially available. It is sufficient for the animals to be given access to the bath once daily. Some breeders will replenish the sand bath from time to time and then replace the sand completely after a few weeks, when it has become soiled through urine and droppings. Droppings should be removed frequently by sifting the sand.

The activities of the animals in the sand eventually create a thin dust layer throughout the breeding room that can be removed with a relatively quiet vacuum cleaner. The actual cleaning frequency (i.e., once a week, once every four weeks, etc.) of the room depends on the amount of dust accumulated. Attempting to wipe the dust off with a damp rag increases the humidity and is not very effective in removing any dust.

Quartz sand and sea sand, even when very fine, are not suitable for bathing. I have seen with my own eyes that these sand grains have sharp edges that, when such a bath is reluctantly used by the animals, virtually grind down the fine hairs of the chinchilla pelt. The sand bath is eventually used up through sand being carried away in the fur of the animals and through contamination with urine and droppings. Consequently, it should be dumped out and replaced every three to four weeks. Here it should also be mentioned that adult chinchillas that are to be mated should be given the same sand bath for some time prior to the anticipated mating. This way the animals get to recognize each other's scent and thus become familiar with each other, reducing or eliminating subsequent fighting.

If one occasionally sees a chinchilla that is conspicuously dark, almost black, and even the normally white abdominal region is dark, then there is a justifiable suspicion that graphite has been mixed into the bathing sand. This is sometimes done to cover up a yellow or brown tinge and is intentional fraud. Slate powder, which gives a bluish color to the fur, is also occasionally used by unscrupulous dealers.

Comparative trials have shown that chinchillas need a sand bath. If this is denied, their fur will quickly become matted. Thus the sand serves to clean it. Contrary to common belief that matting of the fur is caused by its becoming too oily, matting seems to have other causes. At least, it is generally understood that chinchillas do not have any fat glands, so the fur can not become greasy, even though it may look like it.

It has been observed that some animals show little or no interest in a sand bath, the bath remaining largely unused. The reason for this behavior is unknown. On the other hand, animals that usually like to sand bathe and then suddenly refuse to enter the bath are cause for concern: they may well have a health problem. Here it must be emphasized that continuous observation of the entire stock is of paramount importance and should become second nature to anyone keeping chinchillas. The success or failure of chinchilla breeding depends to a

The young chinchilla on the weighing scale is about two days old.

large degree on close observations of the animals and their behavior.

One of the essential equipment items for a properly run chinchilla breeding facility is an accurate scale, preferably one utilizing a sliding weight allowing the weight of the container to be adjusted with tare weights to indicate the correct net weight. Each subsequent weight should be carefully recorded in graph form (weight versus time in weeks or months). Somewhat faster to work with are spring balances or the newer electronic scales. Beginning hobbyists are strongly advised to maintain a regular weighing schedule for all animals. Approximately every 10 to 14 days and just before feeding time is best. This gives a fairly accurate indication of whether the animals are being given a correct diet to promote normal growth.

The weight/time curve for males is fairly even once they are fully grown. In the young the weight curve increases rather steeply up to the age of one year and then slows down. In pregnant females the weight does not increase substantially until about four to six weeks into the pregnancy and continues to increase right up to parturition. These weight curves provide information as to whether a particular animal needs more food or whether it should be put on a diet. Weight curves also indicate a formerly pregnant female has aborted by showing when the anticipated weight increase suddenly comes to a halt, something that would otherwise probably go unnoticed.

For obvious reasons it should not need to be stressed that the room that houses the breeding stock must be kept as clean as possible. This may not be very easy, since the animals continuously create dust that precipitates onto the walls and floor. This dust should be removed often with a vacuum cleaner. The tops of the cages should be brushed off every few days. The cages themselves must be frequently and thoroughly cleaned with a brush and water containing a non-poisonous and odorless detergent. Before the animals are reintroduced the cages must be completely dry. For that purpose it is advisable to have back-up cages on hand so that the animals are not unduly disturbed.

An animal room must be bright and well-ventilated. Although advertisements and some unscrupulous dealers may insist that chinchillas can be kept in a garage or basement, and indeed they may "survive" there for a while, one should not expect any progeny from these animals. It is important to accommodate chinchillas only in a room that gets a lot of sunlight. In fact, I have seen chinchillas clearly enjoying the late afternoon sun. Daylight can be supplemented with suitable fluorescent lighting developed specifically to promote growth in plants maintained in greenhouses. If one extends the daylight hours with artificial lighting this simulates to the animals the onset of spring and so initiates mating.

Seamless floor covering such as linoleum prevents dirt from accumulating in floor cracks. Once a week the floor should be damp-mopped; do not use a wet mop as it is important that the humidity is not increased too much. If the room is ventilated at the same time (to avoid an increase in humidity) care must be taken to avoid the development of a draft.

With this we come to a piece of equipment that is found in many chinchilla breeding facilities, a hygrometer. It indicates the relative humidity in the room. There are also hygrometers that print out humidity values; these are referred to as hygrographs or recording hygrometers.

Anyone closely monitoring his animals will soon recognize that chinchillas are rather sensitive to high humidities — such as during fog and rainy periods — and they are clearly less active then than during a dry weather period. Yet there is little gained from this observation unless something is done about it. This is really only possible by means of air conditioner and dehumidifier units. It is clearly advantageous for the well-being of the chinchillas and possibly also for their pelt quality improvement when the air in their environment (breeding room) is kept dry. This can also be accomplished by means of chemical substances (desiccants), but no matter how it is done, dehumidifying is always costly and anyone buying such equipment may well find that it jeopardizes any anticipated profits from increased pelt production. For that very reason, and based on my own experiences, I consider dehumidifying units unnecessary. I have kept my animals at an elevation of only 300 m in a distinctly damp swampy climate with winter temperatures down to -40°C and summer temperatures up to 40°C without any heating or air conditioning, yet they did rather well. Due to the high operating costs of such equipment, American breeders have largely stopped using it.

From the beginning, you should set up the animals in a dry and bright, draft-free room where they are not disturbed. Some garages may be satisfactory, but dark rooms or damp basements and cellars are totally unsuitable under any circumstances. Some unscrupulous dealers may insist that this is not so just in order to make a quick sale, but they are wrong.

For large chinchilla stocks it usually becomes necessary to build a special breeding shed using timber or bricks, as is commonly done in the United States. It is important when such plans are formulated to include consideration for future expansions. Breeding or pelting sheds erected as a frame construction covered with corrugated iron or tar paper and insulated with fiberglass or similar substances can have a floor area of about 6 by 12 m. The sides can be of timber or Masonite, with glass or clear plastic windows. The important thing is that such a shed protect against rain and snow and be draft-free.

Far more difficult to solve is the question of heating. Generally both species of chinchillas can take cold in our latitudes far better than the summer heat. It is important, therefore, that the room or shed for these animals is well insulated. This would then eliminate the need for heating. The cold tends to improve pelt development, particularly for animals designated for skinning, but this is not altogether true for breeding stock. In chinchillas as well as in golden hamsters, rats, mice, and guinea pigs, it has been observed that reproductive activities decline during the cold months when the indoor temperature drops. For that reason some breeders who want to maintain normal breeding activities all year prefer to heat their facilities when the outside temperature drops below 12°C. A temperature of 15 to 18°C should be maintained inside the breeding room. Rooms that house animals designated for skinning can have lower temperatures. It is, however, important that all rooms are well ventilated and have an adequate oxygen supply.

Here it appears relevant to quite emphatically point out the inherent danger of fire during the heating period. Regrettably, it happens only too frequently that chinchilla breeding facilities go up in flames, causing substantial losses in money and animals. This often leads to public appeals in trade journals for donations to provide a fresh start for those unfortunate breeders. I can only recommend double caution: avoid any potential fire hazards and take out fire insurance, which often is not very expensive.

In the wild, subadult and adult chinchillas can take low temperatures, but these must not fall below freezing. Below freezing temperatures in captivity result in their drinking bottles or automatic watering systems freezing over, and the animals would have to go thirsty.

Pregnant chinchilla females that are close to full term must have supplementary heat. If the breeding room has a temperature of 18°C, a coconut fiber mat should be placed on the bottom of the cage in order to keep out the cold coming from below the cage. This also facilitates littering. Other breeders prefer to place a nest box equipped with a weak incandescent light bulb (5 to 15 watts) into the cage of pregnant females a few days before the anticipated litter date. Far simpler to use is a low-wattage heating pad or plate with a thermostat. Set the dial so the pad becomes barely warm to the touch. This setting requires very little electricity but facilitates drying of the young after parturition. It is certainly worthwhile, because low temperatures in the breeding

The electrical cord of this nest box is safe from being chewed. Once the hinged door of the nest box is closed the incandescent light bulb is beyond the reach of the litter or the parents.

room — especially at a time when females give birth — are the main causes of juvenile mortalities. It need not be stressed that such hot pads must be amply protected so that they and the associated electric cable can not be chewed on by the chinchillas. This is best accomplished by using armored cables. Electricity consumption to achieve a temperature of about 15°C is approximately 12 watts. Such hot pads are commercially available from accessory firms that advertise in trade journals.

Catching and restraining a chinchilla is usually done by the base of the tail, where the animal has strong muscles. The animals should not be left dangling for very long, however, and pregnant females must NEVER be held in this manner. It is just as easy to support the animal from below with one hand while the other hand holds on to the base of the tail. This is a matter of skill and practice for both the breeder and the animals. The animal to be caught must not be chased around the cage. If an animal can not be caught, it is easy to herd it gently into a trap or a nest box where it can be picked up without frightening it. By nature chinchillas are not aggressive and they usually do not bite, but occasionally there are animals that can inflict severe injuries. These are invariably animals that have been ruined through improper handling, and it is usually difficult to hand-tame such animals again. If an animal is known to be aggressive it can be handled with heavy leather gloves.

However, even the most placid chinchilla will become aggressive when its ears are being tattooed. In order to be protected against the rodent's sharp teeth, it is advisable to wear gloves. Animals to be tattooed can also be placed in a small wooden box that closes tightly above. In order to apply the tattoo, the ears are then pulled up through two holes in the lid.

An important element for the well-being and health of chinchillas is lots of exercise. Therefore, sitting boards (platforms) are attached to the sides in the upper half of the cage or enclosure. These boards are eagerly used by the animals, and the jumping required to get up and down affords lots of exercise. As chinchillas show an inclination to chew on the platforms, the boards must be periodically replaced with new ones.

For display in shows, chinchillas are placed in small cages that are just large enough to give the animal enough room to move. Since the size of chinchillas is uniform, it is not necessary for me to provide the dimensions. This also applies to traveling cages. Those used for air transport are usually made of thin plywood or cardboard with wire mesh support and partitions between individual animals. Rail transport permits the use of sturdier boxes made of 10 mm thick timber boards with a wire mesh front only on one side in order to avoid drafts.

Announcements about upcoming shows are found in trade and professional journals. Those who are interested in learning more about chinchillas, from beginning hobbyists to experienced breeders, are strongly encouraged to visit these shows because the animals on display afford an excellent opportunity for comparisons. Moreover, it gives breeders the added opportunity for personal contacts and the exchange of new ideas. One has to keep in mind, though, when visiting such shows that prize-winning animals do not necessarily pass on their favorable characteristics to their progeny. Nevertheless, the acquisition of an attractive stud buck can contribute significantly to the average quality of the progeny. However, experience with other fur-bearing animals has shown that the skins that fetch high prices are not always progeny from prize-winning stud material.

There can really be no strong objection to boarding newly purchased animals with the vendor until the new owner can house them himself. This is common practice in the fur and domesticated animal trade. It is advisable, though, to insist on a written agreement that says essentially that certain animals identified with a particular tattoo are the property of the new owner, and that the vendor retains responsibility for these animals until taken over by the buyer or, alternatively, in case of any losses the vendor will provide replacement animals of equal value. While this may appear self-explanatory, many beginning hobbyists have paid dearly by not insisting on such an agreement.

On the other hand, unlimited boarding of animals with the vendor is unacceptable. Anyone believing he can make a quick profit this way will quickly learn that this is not so, and that indeed he should have purchased shares on the stock market; after all, live animals are not company shares. Even a litter or breeding guarantee from the vendor does not make any difference. A vendor can not give any guarantees that a pregnant female will actually produce a litter, although this is—regrettably — commonly done by unscrupulous vendors. On the other hand, there is nothing wrong with selling a female as being pregnant when indeed it is pregnant. Whether it actually gives birth as well as the size of the litter must not become part of a guarantee. Unfortunately, there was much abuse in this area during the early days of chinchilla breeding, which has not done much to enhance the image of chinchilla breeding, because there are always those who fall victim to this sort of business practice and are persuaded to buy animals of questionable quality.

Anybody who is not able to look after chinchillas himself should invest his money elsewhere.

There have also been instances where importers have masqueraded as breeders and have offered to buy back from the buyer any progeny of a certain age at a fixed price. These vendors may have been able to meet such obligations for a while, but sooner or later financing became too much for them so that the plans and calculations of the buyer collapsed, a possibility that should have been obvious from the start of such a transaction. It would have been wiser for the buyer to keep the progeny himself! Guarantees and arrangements of this type have led without exception (even with other fur-bearing animals) invariably to bankruptcies and severe financial losses for the buyer.

It is a good rule not to enter into this sort of agreement or similar promises, but instead to retain a realistic, level-headed attitude. Breeding chinchillas for pelt production can indeed be an economically viable proposition, but this does not justify people going heavily into debt and buying as many animals as possible, which has actually happened.

In order to start up a chinchilla breeding group it does not matter whether the initial breeding stock comes from a dealer or a breeder. What is important, however, is that the price for these animals is in line with their apparent quality.

In this context I remember the conversation I had with a lady who had sold valuable shares and bought chinchillas with the money. She had boarded the animals and was advised some time later that her animals had died. Then she came to me for advice. I asked her, "If someone told you that you could make a lot of money dealing in diamonds, would you buy a quantity of diamonds without knowing anything about them?" As expected, she said, "No, because I don't know anything about diamonds." When I told her that it is easier to learn how to evaluate precious stones than evaluating chinchillas, she was indeed surprised...unfortunately too late.

Many German chinchilla farms are still early in their development and their animal stocks are small. Although it can not be said that chinchillas — unlike rabbits, mice, and rats — are excessively fertile, they do produce progeny, and sooner or later more cages and more space for housing are needed. This should be taken into consideration from the beginning. Moreover, it has to be remembered that as the stock increases so do the time and effort required to look after the animals. To care for just a few breeding groups can still be fun and is certainly no problem. However, as the facility grows to 50 or more breeding groups it becomes a rather labor-intensive effort. This then raises the question: how many animals can be looked after by a single person? Experience has shown that the limit is about 500 animals per day per adult — not only during the week but on weekends also. Consequently, without a competent replacement there can be no vacation for the dedicated chinchilla breeder.

For European conditions, a breeding facility with about 500 animals, including bucks, is considered to be large. In Germany (FRG) the upper limit is about 1000 animals, while there are even larger chinchilla farms in Denmark, Sweden, and Norway. These are overshadowed by chinchilla farms in North America, where the average size is about 2000 females, while the upper limits are somewhere around several thousand animals. One of these medium sized farms is the Yosemite Fur Farm, Inc., of Oakhurst, California. It is located near the famous Yosemite National Park in the Sierra Nevada, which has peaks in excess of 4,000 m above sea level. The favorable climate in this region was the reason for establishing several large chinchilla breeding farms there and relocating some there from other regions.

The 2000-some females are housed in a shed 45 m long by 9.6 m wide of frame construction on a concrete slab that is 15 cm thick. The outside walls are of weather-proof cedar (2.5 cm thick x 30 cm wide), a material that is locally cut and therefore cheap. Around the entire shed along the upper margin there is a band of 10 x 18 cm hatches of frame construction with clear plastic covers 0.5 mm thick that can be opened for ventilation. The clear plastic cover material also permits adequate light levels during the day. The roof is covered with corrugated aluminum panels, with a layer of Masonite panels (12.7 mm thick) underneath as insulation. Beyond that, the shed is insulated against heat and cold only by heavy construction cardboard.

Coston C. Crouse writes that his chinchillas have endured -32°C and a high humidity without any problems. Experience has shown that the best breeding results are usually obtained at temperatures from 13 to 18°C. In order to maintain an average temperature of 14.4°C during the breeding season, the air of the shed was heated with bottled gas by heaters installed along the narrow sides of the shed. They gave off sufficient heat into this long room so that newborn young could not catch cold. If there had been higher humidities, more heat would have had to be provided. The relative humidity in this region of California varies from 5 to 30%, which is relatively low. Two evaporative coolers are installed along the narrow walls in order to keep the temperatures below 27°C during the summer.

(When I was working — on behalf of someone else — with three Brevicaudata pairs in Minnesota during 1931-32, we often had midday temperatures of 40°C during the summer. Since there was no possibility of providing any cooling for the animals, I had to watch helplessly as they lay on their sides suffering from the heat. Yet they recovered very quickly when the temperature dropped during the evening. This farm was at an elevation of 300 m above sea level.)

Along both sides of the central passage there are polygamous breeding cages arranged in three rows above each other. They are made of point-welded wire with a mesh width of 12.7 x 25.4 mm along the front and back of each cage. Cages for the females are 61 cm long x 38 cm wide x 38 cm high. Above and behind these cages are the passages from which the bucks have access to three to ten females.

A clear plastic container with a lid is attached to the outside front of each cage; it contains the pellets. These handy feed dispensers are replenished once a week with pellets (1.6 mm thickness) manufactured according to an in-house formula. Gravity keeps pulling the pellets downward so the animals have a constant supply of fresh food and there are no leftovers. The only other item on the front of each cage is a door (18 x 23 cm) that is closed with a simple wire catch.

Suspended along the back wall of each cage are little boxes that are open at the top and filled with hay and other roughage, especially fresh bean straw. Each box

A wire floor allows air to circulate freely and any debris that can foul the cage's bottom falls down into a tray lined with woodshavings.

extends across the entire width of the cage and up to about two-thirds of its height. Once filled it holds a supply for about one week for one female. If more pellets or hay is needed, this will be easily spotted just by walking along the cage rows, and the dispenser or hay rack can be quickly replenished. An automatic watering system is installed to serve all the cages. It consists of a 25 mm in diameter plastic tube and automatically closing valves projecting into each cage. The water is supplied from containers attached to the narrow sides and replenished as needed.

White pine shavings are used as bedding: this material soaks up all wetness and is changed only four times a year, which seems to me to be insufficient. Each enclosure contains a sand bath with a 12 cm wide entrance; it is accessible to the animals at all times.

The entire facility is largely automated in order to save labor. In some respects it is reminiscent of automated egg production facilities. Such large operations are impressive but in no way superior to small facilities as far as animal quality is concerned. After all, owners of small facilities are better able to monitor and observe all of their animals.

At this point it may be of interest to the reader to learn about an experiment made with an open-air shed by Eric D. Gunter, manager of the National Chinchilla Breeders of Canada, in which he kept newly weaned young as well as animals designated for skinning. The summer temperatures in his area vary from 24 to 32°C, with occasional peaks in July and August as high as

Pet chinchillas can be permitted to take their sand bath outside the cage several times a week. A cat litter box is an ideal receptacle; easy to clean, store, and inexpensive.

38°C. Winter temperatures from -23 to -24°C are not exactly rare, so the climatic conditions of this area of Canada are rather similar to those of central Europe. Unfortunately, his only reference to the relative humidity is that it is sometimes rather high during the summer.

Gunter's open-air shed is 30 m long and 3 m wide. Wooden posts are rammed into the ground in intervals of 1.2 m. The roof is covered with aluminum sheets, as is common for agricultural buildings in North America. The distance between the lower edge of the roof and the ground is 107 cm. During the winter month the sides — covered with hexagonal wire — are covered to keep out excessive cold and snow. The material used is wire-reinforced plastic sheeting available in rolls. Since this is an open-air building it must have at least some protection against adverse weather during the winter.

The cages are suspended in a single row along the long sides of the building. They are made of spot-welded wire mesh with wire bottoms of smaller mesh. The bedding used is sawdust, wood shavings, straw, peat moss, hay and chaff, wood wool, and pulverized clay dust. It was noted that a wire bottom completely without bedding is the most effective situation because here the droppings fall through to the ground where they are easily removed. Since there was a permanent flow-through of fresh air there was no fly plague during the warm season.

It should be noted here that the opinions of experienced breeders in regard to cage and enclosure bottoms are far from uniform. While some insist that the animals must have bedding, others reject this and instead recommend wire bottoms of smaller mesh that are easy to keep clean. It also must be remembered (and few people ever think of this when they start keeping chinchillas) that wood shavings are not always readily available, and they must also be removed when the enclosures are cleaned out. It need not be stressed that wood shavings used as bedding must be fresh and clean. Since chinchillas sometimes gnaw on shavings, it is imperative that they are not from impregnated, dyed, or polished wood and that they are not contaminated with other foreign materials (plastics, etc.); this could easily cause mortalities. Only soft wood shavings should be used, not wood shavings from potentially poisonous larch or tamarack. Similarly, wood shavings from oak and beech should be rejected because of their high tannic acid content. Wood shavings from very resinous woods are totally unsuitable.

Over a period of three years there were no losses due to heat stroke among the animals kept in this shed. Their health was better than in animals kept under any other condition. But such an open-air shed is not suitable for breeding purposes, because mating takes place later in the year when there is the danger that newborn young can have respiratory problems during cold nights. It is really only necessary to cover the cage bottoms with hay as protection against the cold during winter months. Nest boxes are not required for subadults and for animals designated for skinning. In order to keep out rats and mice that would feed on food tossed out of cages by the chinchillas, it is advisable to introduce a cat. By the way, a cat would not attack escaped chinchillas.

Gunter concludes that such an open-air shed is inexpensive to erect and provides a satisfactory environment for both the animals and those who have to look after them. He has been using such a shed for six years now. The only objection against this type of construction is that it is relatively expensive if the cages are set up in a single row only, rather than stacking three or four rows above each other. This problem could be solved by a slightly different construction technique.

Nutrition

The decisive factor in providing proper nutrition for chinchillas is an understanding of their life in the wild. We know that they live in areas with sparse plant growth. The smaller and more common species, *Chinchilla lanigera*, appears to have lived in the lower-lying areas of Chile. Alfred Brehm reports that in 1829 a traveler named Bennett saw thousands of chinchillas in the course of a day on his rides along the west coast of South America. They are also supposed to have been exceedingly numerous in Peru and Bolivia.

At higher elevations, about 3,000 m above sea level, *C. lanigera* was presumably replaced by the larger type, *C. chinchilla boliviana*. To this day it occurs occasionally at these elevations. A breeding farm, the Criadero Atahualpa S.A., located at an elevation of about 3,300 m above sea level about 1,800 km from Santiago de Chile, has been in operation for some years using this species.

The third type, referred to as Chinchilla Real by the fur-trade, is, according to the sparse information available, an occupant of the highest reaches. Presumably it has always been rather rare and now appears to be extinct.

There are few differences in the lives of these three chinchilla taxa. As occupants of arid desert-like and mountainous terrain they are by nature undemanding. After all, they have to survive on plants available in these areas, and to culture these plants domestically is virtually impossible. This problem has been discussed at length in trade journals in articles written by the Chilean physician and chinchilla breeder Dr. Juan Grau. As valuable as his data are, they are really only of academic interest to the practical chinchilla breeder.

Our knowledge of the precise nutritional requirements of chinchillas is not yet very comprehensive, and it will take some time before more relevant information and experiences have been gained. Some research has been done on this subject in the United States. If one considers the fact that there are still unanswered questions about the nutrition of domesticated animals such as fowl, sheep, cattle, and pigs, it does not come as a surprise that there is still much to be learned about the correct chinchilla diet. There are a variety of pellets available that are essentially chinchilla food ingredients compressed into a pill-like shape. These pellets consist primarily of pure ground-up hay, ground-up lucerne, wheat germ, bran, and other, sometimes secret, ingredients. These pellets are marketed under different names and they are apparently eagerly taken by chinchillas, but I am not sure whether this one-sided diet is adequate in the long run. After all, high juvenile mortalities in some facilities, developmental abnormalities, inadequate milk supply in lactating females, and fur biting are all indications that there are nutritional deficiencies in the diets of these animals. Presumably they do need some green food. This opinion is shared by experienced American breeders, who daily give their animals some freshly cut grass. A sort of temporary solution — especially during the winter — consists of feeding dried greens. In comparison to the hay commonly fed to chinchillas, dried greens contain lots of protein, carotene, and minerals that can be considered to enrich the diet. In many countries this type of food is harvested more and more during rainy summers.

It seems obvious that it is best to feed breeding stock with this type of enriched food. In fact, as far as this author knows, various trials have already been made but details are not yet available. For the same reason, it seems advisable to feed this type of food as a supple-

THE WORLD'S LARGEST SELECTION OF PET, ANIMAL, AND MUSIC BOOKS.

.F.H. Publications publishes more than 900 books covering many hobby aspects (dogs, ats, birds, fish, small animals, music, etc.). Whether you are a beginner or an advanced obbyist you will find exactly what you're looking for among our complete listing of books. or a free catalog fill out the form on the other side of this page and mail it today.

. CATS . . .

. . . BIRDS . .

. . . ANIMALS . . .

. . . DOGS . . .

. . FISH . . .

. . . MUSIC . . .

For more than 30 years, *Tropical Fish Hobbyist* has been the source of accurate, up-to-the-minute, and fascinating information on every facet of the aquarium hobby.

Join the more than 50,000 devoted readers worldwide who wouldn't miss a single issue.

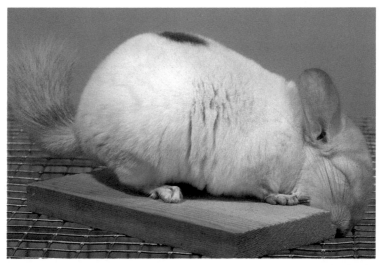

A chinchilla that is predominantly white with a single spot on the back. Unusual mutations find very little favor among commercial chinchilla breeders.

A pure white chinchilla will make an appealing pet. In comparison to white mink fur white chinchilla is considered inferior by chinchilla breeders.

mentary item when the regular green food becomes unavailable. Milk cows will feed on it eagerly, but caution is still advisable. Initially dried greens should be tried out on one or only a few animals for a few weeks before the entire stock is given this food. Always remember that this is a type of enriched food that chinchillas require — and should be given — only in very small amounts.

While scientific observations and practical trials have defined the nutritional requirements for domesticated animals with some degree of certainty, reliable experimental results for chinchillas are still virtually nonexistent. It is quite understandable that some breeders feed too much protein in the form of clover or lucerne hay as well as grain in order to assure that their animals do as well as possible. But instead, chinchillas actually should only be given moderate amounts of protein-rich food. They feed mainly on roughage, so their stomach and intestine are always well-filled.

Pellets or compressed pills made of dried greens (artificially dried grass) have also been commercially available for some time now. It is important that the animals get this type of food as fresh as possible, so it is not advisable to stockpile large amounts of it.

When the breeding stock consists of several hundred animals it is of course much easier to feed pellets, particularly so when automatic feeding devices (feed hoppers) are used. These are of the same type as used for poultry feeding and hold a one-week food supply. Replenishing hoppers is done from the outside of the cage, without having to open the cage door.

It is, of course, important not to fall into the trap of keeping chinchillas too lean, because like other rodents they must always be able to keep their jaws busy. This can best be achieved by giving high-quality dry hay, which must always be available to the animals either di-

In a row of cages on a chinchilla farm shown here hay is placed outside in a shallow trough between individual compartments. This setup dispenses with having to open each cage in order to provide fresh hay.

rectly on the cage bottom or from a hay rack inside the cage.

As easy and time-saving as such devices are for breeders and their animals, there are those who reject them. Some breeders simply feel that using them tends to lessen the breeder's task to continuously observe and monitor his animals. Feeding time is one of the best opportunities to assess the animals response to the diet and observe their behavior. If the feeding dish is always full — for years on end filled with the same pellets — then the animal's feeding drive and food expectation are gone; these are psychological factors that must not be underestimated.

This mutation, also produced on a chinchilla farm, is called brown velvet. Note the color of the eyes, red, quite distinct from the black eyes of the standard gray chinchilla.

Facing page: Nestled comfortably on the arms of an experienced handler are three chinchilla color varieties (beige, gray, and black) that are bred commercially. Note the breeding collar on the female beige chinchilla.

Anyone who has ever kept chinchillas, feeding them every day, preferably twice daily, knows how exactly these animals know their feeding times and how they look forward to them. Of course those who breed chinchillas only on a part-time basis and are able to attend to their animals only at night after work have really no other choice: if they are to look after their animals properly, automatic feeding and watering devices are largely essential. This also applies to most other facilities once the breeding stock has increased to a certain level. There are certain parallels here with the so-called broiler chicken factories, where feeding is done virtually on an assembly line.

Research conducted by Dr. Loeschke at the University of Wisconsin has provided a compilation of nutritive ingredients that can be described as being satisfactory for young animals and breeding stock as well as for those designated for skinning. These ingredients are listed merely for the reader's information, without giving any specific recommendations:

Ground-up clover hay	50%
Wheat bran	15%
Wheat germ meal	20%
Linseed meal	5%
Skinned milk powder	3%
Molasses	3%
Lard (presumably pork fat)	2%
Vitamin A and D*	1%
Di-calcium phosphate (dietary calcium)	0.5%
Iodine salt	0.5%
Vitamin E**	0.1%

*) 2250 I.U. Vitamin A and 300 I.U. Vitamin D, soya meal-based

**) 40,000 I.U. Vitamin E per kilogram

Because of the limited shelf-life of wheat germ, pellets manufactured according to this formula can only be kept for short periods of time. This is also indicated by the fact that vitamin E supplements are recommended.

Beginning chinchilla hobbyists are strongly advised to adhere unequivocally to the feeding instructions given by the supplier of their animals, because chinchillas are quite sensitive to sudden dietary changes. Therefore, any change-over to a different diet should only take place very gradually. This, however, requires a certain experience not expected from beginners. Usually when animals are purchased it is customary for the vendor to also supply some food and the address of the manufacturer or supplier of this type of food. Today it is common practice to feed pellets possibly supplemented with small amounts of grain (about one heaped teaspoon per animal per day).

Beyond that, there are still more widely divergent experiences and opinions as to what constitutes the correct diet for chinchillas than for other domesticated animals. Beginners are advised not to give in to a recommended change of diet or to experiment with the diet of their animals. It is always best to adhere to the instructions given at the time the animals were purchased.

It must be noted here that there are successful American breeders who do not feed pellets, but instead provide the different dietary components in their natural form.

Chinchillas, as strictly herbivorous rodents, require mainly high-quality hay, that is, common meadow, clover, and/or lucerne hay, and also pea or bean straw. It is a common sight to see the animals go first for the dried blossoms, because these seem to taste better and probably also because they contain the essential nutrients in greater proportions. Just as is common practice with regular food, roughage should also be changed frequently from one type of hay to another. This is particularly important for protein-rich clover hay, which con-

A male chinchilla with the genital area exposed. The penis is situated at a considerable distance from the anus.

Left: Genital area of a female chinchilla. The transverse slit between the anus and the urethral papilla is the vaginal opening. *Right:* Appearance of the genital area of a female that has just dropped a litter and is ready to mate again.

The parents of this young beige female chinchilla is indicated by code on the breeding card shown here. A chinchilla, if to be used as a breeder must have a record of its ancestry.

tains too many nutrients and not enough fiber. Similarly, a one-sided diet with lucerne hay (alfalfa to the American breeder) is certainly not advisable.

It is absolutely imperative that all hay given to chinchillas has a fresh smell: it must never give off a damp, musty or moldy odor. Even during short storage periods at times of high humidity, fungus can quickly develop in hay. This can be lethal (and often is) to chinchillas, leading to substantial losses. Therefore, it is particularly important that hay is always stored where it is well-ventilated and dry in order to avoid undesirable surprises. If this is not really possible, one or two days of hay rations should be re-dried before feeding it to chinchillas.

In 1850, a clover-like weed was imported into California from Chile that not only proved to be a valuable food plant but also had favorable effects on the soil. This was lucerne, which the Americans call alfalfa; there are a number of other common names for it, but its scientific name is *Medicago sativa*. Since then, lucerne has become an important food item in agriculture as well as for breeding chinchillas. Its average protein content is 14.3%. It also has a high level of calcium, 1.43%, which is important for pregnant and nursing females; much carotene (provitamin A); and substantial amounts of vitamin D, more than any other food plant.

Hay must be given fresh daily. Any left over from the previous day must be removed; usually these are merely the wooden stalks, which have little nutritional value. The term "hay" commonly refers to meadow hay; this should be given in ample amounts. Clover and lucerne hay must only be offered in small amounts.

The most convenient and effective way to feed hay is in a suspended wire hay rack, which can easily be made by anyone handy with simple tools. This forces the animals to exercise when pulling hay from the rack. If hay is simply placed on the cage floor the animals will quickly trample it down and it becomes soiled. Consequently, using a hay rack is the preferred method. Each animal should get one handful of hay per day. It is convenient to place the hay in the space between two adjacent cages so that the animals have to exercise somewhat while pulling the hay into their cage.

In addition to hay, chinchillas also need grain. They usually do not feed on rye, but wheat, barley, oats, and corn are eagerly taken. Keep in mind that individual animals have different preferences so that you are advised to try different types of grain. Always remember to provide the animals with a varied diet. Since oats and corn have a high nutritional value and the latter also contains rather large amounts of plant fats, it is advisable to be cautious when feeding corn. How much is required by chinchillas is not exactly known, but about one heaped teaspoonful of grain per animal per day is about right. Other seeds such as hemp, sunflower seeds, linseed, and others can also be fed, but due to their high fat content they are not really recommended as chinchilla food.

Beginners are always afraid their animals are not getting enough food, so they usually overfeed. Such concerns are hardly applicable here, since chinchillas are far easier overfed than underfed. The long and dense chinchilla fur gives these animals a larger and more massive appearance than they really are. Weighing a chinchilla reveals that about ½ kg is about the normal weight for both a buck and a female that is not pregnant.

Consequently, one has to remain strong when the animals are hanging at the front cage wire begging for food, especially sweets, because these are quickly converted into excess body fat. It is a common occurrence that it takes longer for progeny to arrive than had been anticipated. As can be seen from letters written by inexperienced breeders to trade journals, the reason for this

If you do not intend to breed your pet chinchillas, it will be best to keep them in separate cages. In the presence of an estrous female, males inevitably fight with one another.

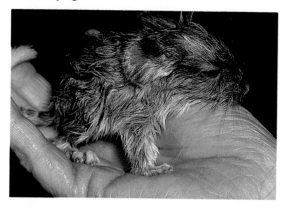

Chinchillas are born with a full coat, open eyes, teeth! and ready to walk.

A mother chinchilla will not object to your handling her new baby, even if still wet like the baby chinchilla shown here.

A litter of two to three is considered the average litter size for chinchillas bred commercially. Individuals that do not measure up to the standards of the breeder are rejected.

is invariably overfeeding. One simply can not expect animals that are excessively fat to breed since their reproductive organs are not functioning.

With time and some sensitivity anyone will quickly learn what correctly fed breeding stock should look like. The feeding practice with other fur-bearing animals such as silver fox and mink is similar: food ration and composition are dependent upon the season; the progeny are given ample food until pelt maturity; the breeding stock is kept lean prior to mating; and even pregnant females are not given too much food until after they have given birth.

At this point it seems to be relevant to make a few comments about yellow fattiness in chinchillas. This is a problem for many tanning operations because a sizable percentage of the skins supplied to the market are stained by yellow fat. Generally such pelts have a thin leather skin that makes tanning difficult. Yellow fattiness is also a significant problem in mink breeding. In mink, the development of yellow fat is presumably due to an uneven ratio between saturated and unsaturated fatty acids that places a burden on liver functions. Apparently this is the same condition referred to as "yellow ears" in chinchillas because the tissue surrounding the auditory passage takes on a distinctly yellow color. Initially this is only weakly indicated, but later it may even change into an orange color. During later stages of this disease, the yellow tinge also appears on the genitals and around the anus. If an animal that shows signs of yellow fattiness is turned over and one blows against the fur along the abdominal region, then the same yellow color is visible there, too. Moreover, the abdomen is often sore and shows doughy swellings. During subsequent stages of this disease the yellow coloration spreads over the entire body and eventually affects the entire skin. Otherwise good quality pelts become unmarketable due to yellow fattiness. Most likely this condition also influences the breeding suitability of the animals.

The main cause for this condition is presumably large amounts of saturated fats in the diet. A preventive measure against yellow fat is a moderate food supply. In daily practice this is easily done by first giving hay, on which the animals can feed as much as they like, before pellets are given.

In his book *Diseases of Chinchillas*, Prof. Dr. Kraft observes that yellow fat in chinchillas occurs when there is a lack of vitamin E. The best method to prevent yellow fat is still a near-natural diet of small amounts of grain, except oats, which lack a living embryo or "germ," and corn, which has a high fat content.

Chinchillas meet their water requirements from desert plants and from dew that accumulates on the leaves of these plants, but they never drink from springs or streams in the wild since these do not exist in their native habitat. Chinchillas are equipped with a sort of natural protective cover, in the form of their exceedingly dense fur coat, against cold and heat, just like the edelweiss and other alpine plants. Even during periods of considerable heat these "living thermos flasks" are certainly not as thirsty as we would be in their surroundings. Interestingly enough, it has been shown experimentally that when edelweiss are transplanted to lower mountain regions, the protective cover against sun and desiccation becomes unnecessary and may be lost. In chinchillas such regressions of the fur coat have not yet occurred, although this is quite conceivable after prolonged captive breeding. Certain genetic deficiencies such as lack of milk and saliva flow may be warning signs of captive maintenance that is not in accordance with the requirements of these animals.

Much has already been said and written about the problem of whether chinchillas should be given drink-

Left: A chinchilla mother will not hesitate to cover her young from a possible danger, like when the cage door is opened for whatever reason. *Below:* Too young to reach the hay rack, these baby chinchillas eat whatever hay is within reach. Remove old and soiled hay and replace with fresh hay routinely.

The sex of a female chinchilla is already evident at an early age. In comparison to a male, the urethral papilla of a female lies very close to the anus. This female is just a week old.

A chinchilla that is unable to nurse, possibly orphaned or rejected by its mother, can be fed artificially. Milk can be dispensed by a liquid dropper at regular intervals.

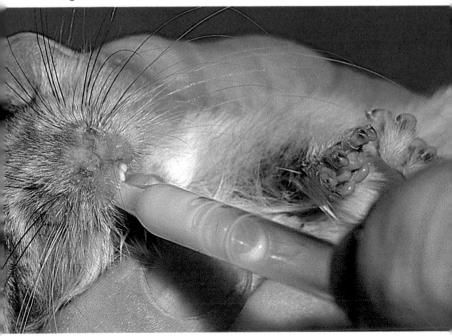

ing water or not. Personally I am convinced they need not be given drinking water. My opinion is based on a one-year trial with three pairs of Brevicaudata, but this presupposes, of course, that the small water requirements of these animals is met by green food or fruit in their diet. The fact that those three pairs that I kept gave birth to young and that these were raised without any lack of milk should be sufficient evidence for this. Yet Lanigera that are kept in the United States and always get drinking water frequently suffer from inadequate lactation — indeed food for thought.

Various breeders who, based upon my experiences and suggestions, have given adequate amounts of green food and fruit instead of drinking water have confirmed that the health and condition of their animals have improved and that there were no longer the familiar and frequent bouts with gastrointestinal diseases. But when chinchillas are fed exclusively on a diet of hay and pellets and no green food, they must, of course, be given drinking water or otherwise they would become dehydrated. A medium sized lettuce leaf or a similar amount of fresh hay (which must not be damp) with every morning and evening feeding is sufficient to meet the water requirements of these animals. More green food may cause soft feces or even diarrhea.

There is also little or no consensus among experienced breeders on the question of whether chinchillas should be given fresh green food or not. Green food is recommended by DeChant, Clarke, Houston and Prestwich, and Parker, all authors of authoritative publications. I share their opinion, since green food is commonly used by poultry and other domesticated animals. It is also generally known that fresh green food has a favorable effect on fertility and well-being because it contains essential substances (minerals and trace elements). Admittedly, giving green food requires a little bit more effort by the breeder, especially when large animal stocks are being kept.

Not every breeder has the opportunity to feed his animals green food that he has grown himself. In any event, it is recommended that Jerusalem artichoke, *Helianthus tuberosus,* be sowed if possible. This plant, which is related to sun flowers, forms highly nutritious tubers in the ground that, together with its leaves, can be fed to chinchillas. Dr. G. A. Kueppers-Sonnenberg reports that feeding Jerusalem artichokes has proved to be effective against constipation. This plant is also used as feed by rabbit breeders.

Those opposed to giving green food to chinchillas point out that large American farms feed only hay and pellets throughout the year. Whether this causes the widely occurring deficiency syndromes has not yet been resolved. I am of the opinion it is certainly a contributing factor to lactating problems, substantial juvenile mortalities, miscarriages, stillbirths, infertility, fur biting, and many other developmental problems.

By the way, chinchillas are not the only animals with unusually low water requirements. For instance, in other desert regions of the world there are rodents that apparently can thrive without any opportunity to drink while exposed to daytime temperatures of 50°C; yet they manage to nurse and raise their young effortlessly, as has been shown by research. Since it rains only every two to three years in those regions, these animals would have long ago died of dehydration had they not been specifically adapted to live in such adverse climates. Whether guinea pigs need water or not is also a question of how they are being kept and fed. If they are given enough hay and green food or if they are permitted to graze at their leisure, they may never touch their drinking water.

It should not have to be stressed that animals that

Left: A chinchilla show is generally open to the public. Attending such a show permits one to examine at close view the latest mutations of importance today.
Below: Chinchillas are housed in special show cages, not too small, just large enough to permit a chinchilla to move around freely.

To compensate for possible deficiencies in your chinchilla's diet, vitamins can be added to the food or water. Liquid vitamins can be given directly through the mouth using a medicine dropper.

A salt spool will satisfy a chinchilla's craving for minerals it may need.

have always received drinking water must not be denied access to water from one day to the next. For that matter, any sudden change in diet such as a sudden transition from a winter to a spring diet must be avoided, because this can cause digestive problems. The best way to proceed is a gradual process; the animals are first given some green food, such as fresh grass or herbs, and still given an opportunity to drink. If the water level in the drinking container is closely monitored it soon becomes apparent that the animals are no longer using drinking water; instead they use the green food to satisfy their water requirements.

It is absolutely imperative not to be misled by other breeders who may suggest a sudden change in diet for your chinchillas. Experience has shown that these animals are clearly sensitive to such changes, which can result in gastrointestinal diseases and possible mortalities. Therefore, it is important, especially for beginners, to stay initially with the original diet for the new animals. This, incidentally, also applies every time new animals are acquired.

The most frequent reason for breeders to change the diet of their animals is juvenile mortalities or poor quality progeny. This precautionary warning, of course, does not preclude occasional dietary experimentation, but such experimentation must never be done on the entire stock, only to individual animals, preferably only to those deemed to be surplus. Only after a trial period of several weeks without any adverse effects can the new diet be extended to the rest of the stock, but again this must also be done gradually.

The amount of food to be given per animal per day can only be indicated approximately, since the precise requirements vary from one animal to the next. Therefore, initially it is better to keep the daily food rations deliberately short and watch the animals as they feed eagerly, rather than giving them too much. Excessive amounts of food invariably lead to soft feces or even diarrhea, which is often difficult to cure. The best evidence of an adequate diet is the droppings, which must always be relatively dry and brittle.

These comments may appear to be too elaborate, but since this topic is of such fundamental importance for the well-being of the animals, I have attempted to document my opinions in considerable detail. Here I should add that some breeders give diluted milk to their animals because they believe that this provides a more complete diet. Yet, since chinchillas in the wild never get milk except the young when they are being nursed, this is not only unnecessary but indeed is counterproductive. Apart from the fact that milk contains large amounts of animal protein and fat, there is also the added danger that the milk turns sour during warm weather, which can cause serious digestive problems.

A German lady who was breeding chinchillas reported that she daily would give all young from the third week on a pinch of yogurt in a small dish. After about a week the animals started to feed on it. These animals weighed 430 to 490 grams during the fourth or fifth month; the ones that had refused to take yogurt weighed only 345 to 380 grams. Once weaned, the young were given half a teaspoon of yogurt at room temperature every other day.

Providing as close as possible natural care and diet in captivity is not only the most sensible approach, but also the healthiest and most effective. If one sticks to the principle of feeding chinchillas on a relatively low-fat, low-protein diet, you will have success. As herbivores, chinchillas also need fresh green food in addition to large amounts of hay. Only when this is not available can the occasional apple be given as a substitute, but it should never be more than about an eighth of an apple

A medicine dropper (above) and an ordinary plastic squeeze bottle (below) are common household items and they can be used in giving medication and anything else in liquid form to a chinchilla.

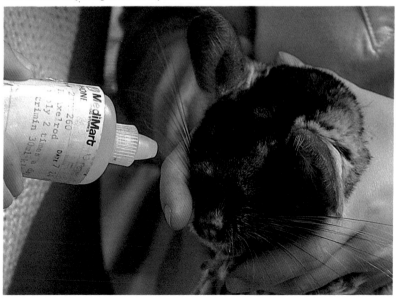

Right: For grooming a chinchilla a metal comb, not a brush, is used. This grooming comb consists of fine-toothed and wide-toothed sections. *Below:* The tuft of fur shown on the left came from a standard gray chinchilla that is normal. On the right is a tuft of fur from a chinchilla that engaged in fur biting.

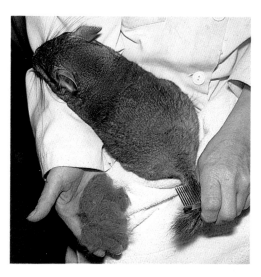

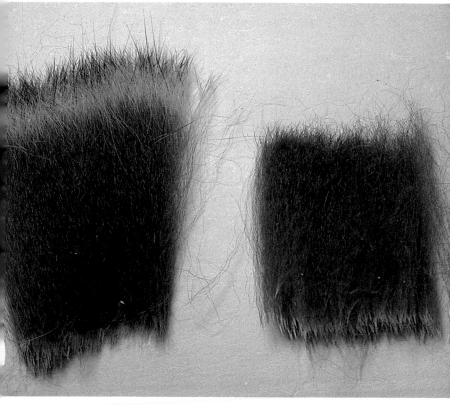

(normal size), of course WITH its peel, per day. The best and cheapest green food is grass that is completely dry. Wet grass (cut during or shortly after rain) can be dangerous for the digestive system. In rabbits and guinea pigs, and also in horses and cattle, this can cause gas, twisting of the bowels, colic, and even death. Therefore, it is important to make sure that grass is really dry but not wilted. Apart from grass, chinchillas can also be given the occasional leaf of lettuce, especially the green leaves, carrot greens as well as the carrots themselves, and celery with leaves, but not the leaves of turnips. Cabbage is unsuitable for chinchillas; in fact, the animals will rarely touch it. In the line of fruit, only pears (apart from apples) are keenly taken, while stone or pitted fruits are not really suitable at all or should be used in an emergency only. After all, this sort of food is not found in the natural habitat of chinchillas. Similarly, almonds and nuts are also not suitable because of their high fat and protein content, even though many chinchillas will eagerly feed on nuts. Instead, it is better to offer occasionally some raisins or other dried fruit; chinchillas seem to be particularly fond of dried carrots. As mentioned in Frederico Albert's monograph, in the wild chinchillas feed on thistles, the fruit of the Indian fig tree (*Ficus indica*), a sort of wild-growing melon, various bulbous shrubs, and also on mosses and lichens. The most preferred item, though, is carob, in particular its seeds. Allegedly chinchillas gather the fruits from carob trees (*Ceratonia siliqua*) and keep them in their burrows, but this type of hoarding behavior, such as displayed by European and Syrian hamsters, has never been seen in captive chinchillas. There is also some doubt whether bulbous plants are part of the natural diet of chinchillas, since these animals are not known to dig and they do not have any digging claws.

This should just about cover all aspects of chinchilla nutrition. Basically, these animals must be given a varied, diversified diet, especially in view of the fact that there are still large gaps in our knowledge of what the specific dietary requirements are and what size ration should be given. Their feeding behavior clearly shows that they appreciate variety in their diet, but also that there are individual preferences.

Advertisements in professional and trade journals show that there are a number of food pellet manufacturers who market their products under particular brand names. Obviously they are doing this to make a profit. Large chinchilla breeding farms have their own machines to manufacture food pellets themselves. In contrast to non-compacted food (hay, grain, and other components), pellets have the definite advantage of reduced wastage by the animals. Some breeders also feed processed oats (oatmeal) to their chinchillas, which I consider to be essentially worthless — apart from the fact that the highly nutritious kernel has been destroyed, especially after a long shelf life, chinchillas have excellent teeth and they like to put them to good use by macerating whole grain feed. This way they get the kernels that are high in vitamin E. Moreover, non-processed grain food has virtually an unlimited shelf life under proper condition and is most certainly cheaper.

Since an inadequate milk supply in nursing females is not particularly uncommon and juvenile mortality is of grave concern to many breeders, this leads to the assumption that the food offered to chinchillas in captivity does not contain all the required nutritional elements and ingredients. In order to avoid this, the diet must be kept varied and the hay used should also come from different regions. Since alpine hay has a particularly pleasant smell and is of high nutritional value, it is recommended that breeders try to get a regular supply.

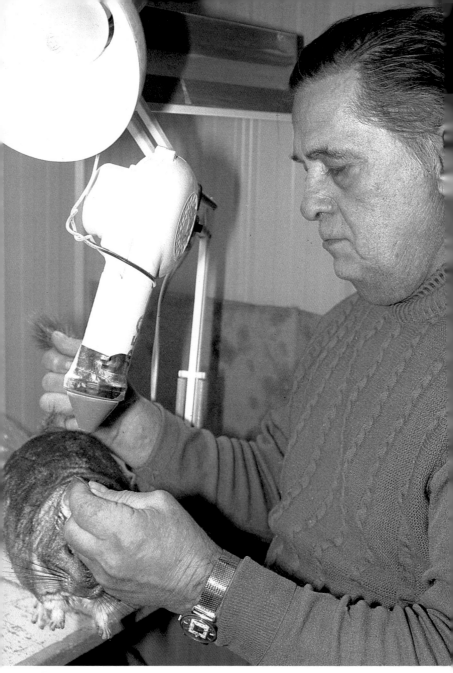

This technician is using an air blower for examining the quality of a chinchilla's coat. A good source of light is indispensable for a proper evaluation of a chinchilla specimen.

These well built housing units for chinchillas are located in England. Good housing ensures protection from the rigors of climatic changes there.

Left: A technician demonstrating the electrical equipment used in the preparation of chinchilla pelts. *Right:* Some of the tools needed in the preparation of chinchilla pelts.

Salt and calcium should be offered as minerals, the former as a salt lick or salt wheel and the latter as a piece of edible chalk, both placed inside the cage. The chinchillas will often be seen chewing on this. Some breeders also place charcoal in the cage and a small block of mineral salts with trace elements such as is used for domesticated animals. Remember that only small quantities of salt and minerals are needed — ingestion of large quantities of salt should be avoided.

Since the teeth in rodents continue to grow throughout the life of the animal, it is absolutely essential that each cage contains a piece of untreated wood, preferably a fresh or dried apple tree branch that can be slowly chewed to pieces. American breeders give their animals a piece of pumice to chew on, but a well-known German breeder who has been very successful with chinchillas rejects this idea categorically and instead places a piece of blown (foam) concrete in the cage. His animals gnaw on this piece of concrete so persistently that it is invariably gone after a few weeks. This is clearly a sign that chinchillas have to grind their teeth down. If they do not have an opportunity to do this on a regular basis the teeth will become too long, which in turn can lead to feeding and nutritional problems.

A scientific formulation for a balanced diet such as is used in commercial poultry farms is not yet available for chinchillas. Therefore, it is absolutely imperative that the animals are closely monitored, that different types of foods and ingredients are tried out (within reason), and that one proceeds with great deliberation. Just as in human nutrition, there is no such thing as a universal diet. One person prefers to eat a lot of fish, another one is a vegetarian, while others need hardly any fruit or vegetables, and some prefer only very little meat. In principle this is the same in chinchillas. The breeder does not have to go to extremes to determine precisely the exact individual food preferences for each one of his animals. Once the breeding stock has grown substantially in numbers, individual attention is no longer possible and the animals will still do well.

It is more difficult to provide detailed comments about the amount of food required by herbivores than for carnivores. The main reason for this is that herbivores tend to scatter their food and leave much uneaten food around. Whether the diet is adequate or not can only be determined by a weight curve, which should be maintained for every breeding animal right from the start based on regular weighing. The only thing that can be said about green food and similar substances (bulbs, fruit) is that these items should only be given in small amounts in order to avoid gastrointestinal problems (diarrhea). It is also important to offer a varied diet. The entire digestive process must be constantly monitored by the appearance of the droppings. Too many yellow turnips, which contain yellow pigments, are alleged to cause the fur to turn yellow.

In a polygamous breeding setup where the male can visit the cage of many females, it is impossible to stop the buck from taking as much food as he wants. For bucks used in an intensive breeding program this is unimportant. Moreover, it would be difficult to control because females with young — particularly the young — must have an adequate and constantly available diet. Essentially then, the weight curve for the buck is the only way of keeping track of how much the male is eating and if it is getting too fat.

Left: A lady who wants to be different in her attire may prefer a chinchilla corsage instead of the usual flower corsage. *Below:* To create a muff to match chinchilla coats requires several pelts that closely match each other in pattern, like the three examples shown.

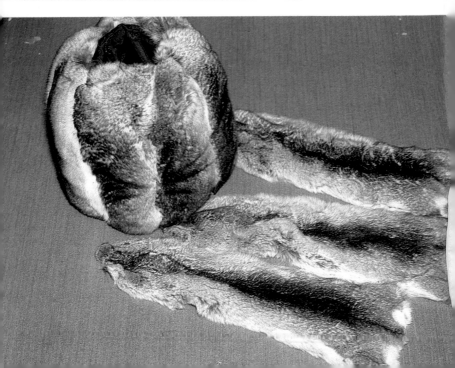

Mutations

Only since the turn of the century has science had at its disposal the knowledge needed to exert economically beneficial influences upon the progeny of plants and animals. This includes means of increasing crop yield, protecting plants against diseases or parasites, increasing milk fat content and milk production in cows, and producing sheep that grow more and better quality wool, just to mention a few examples. Moreover, race horses that excel in speed over the more standard horses and tulips that give us esthetic viewing pleasure are products of decades of selective breeding to produce particular end products desired by man.

There appears to be some sort of contradiction here, since it was stated initially that we have had this knowledge to produce changes only since the turn of the century, while many domesticated plants and animals were developed many centuries ago, but this is not really a contradiction. Ever since man first became a farmer, he has always selected what he deemed to be the best fruit and vegetable to be used as seed for next year's crop and he bred the best sheep and goats to get the best offspring. These were the means by which varieties were developed in domesticated plants and animals, so much so that modern representatives of domesticated plants and animals often have only a remote resemblance to the original types.

One of the best examples of this is the Angora Rabbit. Its ancestor, the gray short-haired wild European rabbit, represents the original form in body shape and fur. But how could the fur change to such a degree that it became white and so much longer and silk-like that it could be spun?

The basic understanding of genetic changes is based on scientific experiments made by the Augustine prelate Johann Gregor Mendel (1822-1884) and published around 1860. These studies were forgotten until redis-covered by De Vries as well as Correns and Tschermak at the turn of the century. While earlier selective breed-ing of plants and animals was very much random and took many generations to reach its goal, an understand-ing of *genetics*, the science of heredity, often allows a breeder to know in advance what will happen when two animals are mated and makes it possible to actually plan a series of breedings to produce a wanted fur or body type.

The study of genetics is quite complicated and many practical breeders have trouble understanding even the basic laws of the science. Instead of spending time here with complicated explanations, I suggest instead that you find a good basic college textbook on genetics and study it in your spare time. Only the most basic termi-nology will be required in this book.

Inbreeding refers to matings within the same line of genetic relationships, such as parents to children, grand-parents to grandchildren, or siblings to siblings. The de-velopment of nearly all pure varieties of domesticated animals is based on inbreeding. To this day there is of-ten still a belief among amateurs that any breeding col-ony must receive "new blood" from time to time by mating to a different line or lineage. This often is true. The prerequisite for successful inbreeding with a spe-cific objective is that both parent animals of the original line be absolutely healthy, otherwise inbreeding will ac-centuate any faults present, such as declining fertility, poor development of young, and lack of milk in nursing females. The resistance against these effects can vary widely between individual families. If particular traits such as fertility, fur color, and fur quality are to be enhanced, inbreeding will achieve this objective in the fastest possible way. The crowning achievement of this breeding method in chinchillas is reduced variability among individual animals, which in turn facilitates good pelt prices. Remember, however, that the original breeding stock must be as fault-free as possible and any defective offspring must not be allowed to breed. Inbreeding does not produce faults, but it will concentrate and accentuate any that are present.

Inbreeding is essential in establishing quantities of a desirable **mutation.** A mutation is a genetic freak that occurs suddenly in a group of animals and is transmissible to the mutant's offspring. Chinchilla breeders are interested in color mutations, some of which are quite attractive and desirable. Thus if an animal with a new and desirable pelt color suddenly appears among normal gray animals, it can be used in a program of inbreeding to establish and even improve the new color in chinchillas.

Some American chinchilla farms and one Polish facility had one of the earliest chinchilla mutations. These were very light, more or less white types, though not albinos because they had dark eyes and in most instances also a partially dark tail.

During recent years there has been a considerable increase in the variety of chinchilla color mutations. Apart from snow-white chinchillas, there now are animals that are velvet black, silver, lilac or blue, and beige. The economic significance of these animals is still fraught with problems.

Many of the white chinchillas now available originate from a buck born on 21 April 1955 in California. It was given the tattoo B7 and named "Whitie." This white mutation, as well as the "pearl-white" types with a pale or lavender blue undercoat, is only of moderate interest for breeding purposes. After all, a snow-white chinchilla coat would not be very attractive, despite its rarity. On the other hand, I have seen pelt samples that have convinced me that animals with such mutations and able to pass on this color in their progeny can be used to develop new color shades that can be of great beauty.

Apparently there are no problems with rearing white chinchillas; they are supposed to be generally strong and healthy. An American breeder reported that his bucks had weighed in excess of 500 g within six months. However, acquisition of white bucks can only be justified for advanced breeders with suitably large breeding stock. Whether chinchilla mutations are of such high value as those occurring among minks can not yet be answered. We will only know the answer to this question once there are sufficiently large pelt assortments coming onto the market and the response from the fashion industry is known.

Another interesting color mutation is Black Velvet, with a coat that looks like black velvet. These animals are used for matings with standard animals. So far it is uncertain whether the fashion industry and fur trade are interested in these unusual and expensive novelties. This also applies to beige-colored mutations, in which some breeders have placed great expectations. Crosses between beige-colored animals and black velvets produce brown velvets, animal with a brown velvet coat. This should be of interest to the trade provided there is a sufficiently large supply, but it will probably take quite some time until mutation pelts achieve economical importance. Whether black chinchilla pelts have a future now seems to be doubtful, especially since recent supplies have become less uniform in color tone, which makes sorting more difficult. Beyond that, I can not imagine that a coat made of black chinchilla pelts is appealing to fashion-conscious women, especially since there are enough other, cheaper black pelts. Beginning breeders are strongly advised against the breeding of mutations, especially since there are still many problems to be solved and answers to be found even in the breeding of standard chinchillas.

The vast majority of all cultivated Lanigera go back to a few animals imported from South America into California by Mathias F. Chapman in 1923. No doubt there were other imports later, but the number of animals involved is not known. There are increasingly frequent reports in recent years in American professional journals about white, black, and spotted chinchilla progeny, such changes being the first signs of what is referred to as domestication; i.e., a change of the wild form into a domesticated animal. So many mutations having already appeared in a species that has only been bred for a few years compared to other domestic animals, certainly leads one to expect many more mutations. Not all of these will be economically desirable, although some may well become important. The latter would probably include long-haired chinchillas, counterparts to the Angora Rabbits, which could supply wool for the spinning of fine garments and cloth.

It is well-known that dogs and some types of poultry have a tendency to produce dwarf and giant forms. This leads to the assumption that chinchillas may eventually produce mutations in respect to their normal size. I would really be interested to find out whether this assumption comes true. Indeed, a Canadian chinchilla farm has already advertised "Jumbo Chinchillas." Regrettably, there was no reply to my enquiry as to whether these were actually giant chinchillas and how much larger they were compared to normal chinchillas. In any event, sometime and somewhere a giant chinchilla strain will probably emerge, and it can be assured of having a great commercial future if the animals have suitable pelt characteristics required by the market.

A pet chinchilla of white mutation.

Good pelts would, after all, be the essential prerequisite, as large pelts of good quality would of course fetch better prices than normal pelts because fewer of them would be required to make a particular garment. If one considers the fact that humans have grown taller during the last half century and you now often see young people who are very much taller than their parents, then the possibility of a giant chinchilla mutation does not seem to be far off. Even improved nutrition may make a significantly larger chinchilla available eventually.

Breeding Chinchillas

Anyone calling himself a real chinchilla breeder has to do more than just increase his stock. The demands placed on him today may not be that great, but experience in other areas of breeding fur-bearing animals has shown that they are growing. Basically, they can be reduced to a rather simple common denominator: *quality,* which is beauty of hair and color related to the size of the pelt. It is absolutely imperative to start out with breeding stock that really deserves the name. Since the reader of this book may have only limited experience with these animals (or none at all), he would probably expect at this stage useful hints about acquiring his first animals, what to look for, and what good breeding animals should look like. This may indeed be easier said than done, as the knowledge to make the distinction between a good chinchilla and a bad one usually comes only with years of practical experience.

But the reader must not despair, especially since many who sell breeding animals hardly know themselves the full breeding potential of the animals — and that may not be all bad. By this I do not mean that we can obtain quality, prize-winning progeny from poor parental stock. It is indeed best to start out with the very finest breeding material available within the financial means of the breeder. Anyone who has decided to start up chinchilla breeding makes his own choices. Therefore, on one hand he should rely on his own judgment, and on the other hand on a little bit of luck. He is not likely to go out and buy just any animal, but instead he will first try to get an overall impression of what chinchilla breeding is all about. It is essentially the same as with any other major decision with far-reaching implications—be it a wedding proposal or the purchase of a car, particularly a used one!

Therefore, first and foremost it is important to have a look at the pedigree papers before a sale is completed; this will provide a fair amount of information about the evaluations of parents and grandparents. There actually are chinchillas for sale that are not worth their feed; they are usually without identification tattoos, and pedigree and evaluation documents usually are not available. As breeding animals these would be too expensive at any price, although they might make fine pets. On the other hand, there are high-quality animals that are either prize-winners or progeny from prize-winning parents; they can cost in excess of a thousand dollars in the United States and may be worth every cent.

Regrettably there is no short-cut to becoming a chinchilla expert, and that includes learning to select and buy chinchillas. Yet, anyone who understands people and is a skilled observer will be able to make the correct decision once he has seen and compared a number of different animals and their owners.

Chinchillas can be purchased from a wide selection of animals available at varied prices directly from breeders or dealers. Pet-quality stock is available at many pet shops. Highly favorable for the future development of chinchilla breeding is the fact that there are already breeders trying to operate their facilities at pelt production quality. These people rarely sell breeding animals, attempting instead to improve the quality and uniformity of their own stocks rather than being tempted to make a quick buck. If one acquires breeding animals with relevant documentation (as is now common practice) one has something of a guarantee of their pedigree quality. Unfortunately, however, there are also breeding certificates of doubtful reliability. If there are any doubts, it is advisable to ask the seller to get the animal re-evaluated and have a new set of papers issued so that there are no regrets later.

Although chinchillas do not reproduce as rapidly as some other rodents, ample planning should go into the housing requirements, including future expansions that may be contemplated as well as the expenses involved, BEFORE the first breeding animals are purchased. When the young are weaned they need cages as well as space for these cages. Although this is self-explanatory, experience has shown that beginners in their initial enthusiasm sometimes completely forget about this. Besides, setting up a breeding facility involves operating funds for cages and other items.

Anyone on a tight budget and with cash flow problems may well decide to recover some or all of his operating expenses initially from the sale of young, rather than building up his breeding stock. This can of course be done, provided he can part with the first young.

Let us suppose matters have progressed to the stage where the new buyer is convinced he has found just the right breeding animals, and they belong to a breeder who appears to be trustworthy. Not only is the fur of these animals flawless, but it is also nicely even in density and color, the eyes are clear and shiny, and the animals are active but not flighty. Then the time has come to work out with the owner when the animals are to be taken over and picked up.

Before the animals are paid for and taken home the new owner must convince himself that he has actually purchased a male and a female. Distinguishing the sexes in chinchillas is no more difficult than in other rodents such as mice or guinea pigs; it only requires a bit of experience and some training. If sexing is not done correctly the new owner may well take two females home and then be surprised when there are no progeny. On the other hand, two bucks would be embroiled very quickly in a fight to the death!

At first sight there appear to be very few differences between the sexes, but a closer look reveals that the distance between the male's penis and the anal opening is larger. In females the anal opening, horizontal slit-like vagina, and opening of the urinary tract are situated close together. Anyone who wants to be quite sure can extrude the male's penis through some downward pressure against the lower abdominal region of the animal. It is best to ask an experienced breeder to demonstrate this technique a few times. Anyone experienced with chinchillas can also sex these animals by the shape of the head and other external features, much as in similar differences between male and female cats.

When a chinchilla is caught and held up by its tail, one can see the anus as it opens at regular intervals and each time a bean-sized yellow nodule becomes visible at the lower corner of the anal slit. Simultaneously there is a peculiar pungent odor that is reminiscent of commercial vitamin B1 (thiamine) preparations. This yellow nodule contains the opening of the anal sac, an observation described and published for the first time by Prof. Dr. H. Kraft. He postulates that this is part of a warning or fright reaction also known to occur in other animals.

Payment for living animals is generally settled in advance. This includes the assumption by the seller of certain obligations; for instance, he guarantees the progeny, possibly for the entire reproductive life of an animal. Beginners like to purchase females that are either pregnant or are known to have conceived, because this virtually guarantees one or more young in due course. Such proven breeding stock can prevent early disappointments that tend to be hardest for anyone starting out with chinchillas. However, those with a tight budget or those unwilling to spend much money may wish to start out with subadults that have not yet bred. This, of course, requires more patience but has the advantages of being cheaper and—more importantly—the seller knows just as little about the breeding potential of these animals as the buyer, who may well come out ahead in such a deal. As always, anyone taking a bigger risk may also possibly reap a greater gain.

If the transit time for such newly acquired animals is short, they need only be protected against rain, snow, or heat. If this involves travel by train or plane, one should take the advice of the vendor and follow all airline or train regulations. The transport cage must be sufficiently large to give the animals ample room for movements. They should also be given sufficient hay and green food. The outside must be clearly marked "LIVE ANIMALS," "MUST PROTECT AGAINST DRAFT," and "DO NOT FEED," plus any other required wording the carrier (plane, train, bus) may insist on.

Everything must be ready for the animals when they arrive so they can be quickly transferred to their new home and will settle down as quickly as possible and adapt to the new surroundings. This is particularly important for pregnant females so that they do not abort. Experience has shown that even pregnant chinchillas can be quite adaptable. It has happened many times that near-term pregnant females have given birth while in transit on an airplane, yet the litter was in good condition upon arrival — often to the consternation of custom officials, since the invoiced number of animals suddenly was no longer correct!

There is little that can be done for newly arrived animals other than leaving them in peace after they have been given food, including green food. First the animals have to orient themselves to see where they are. With constant vibrations of the whiskers, everything is sniffed at and investigated. This is when the first sounds are emitted by the new arrivals. An alert breeder will quickly understand this chinchilla "language" to the extent that he can tell whether the animals are contented or not. This is no doubt a means of communication among these animals. There are both "talkative" and less communicative chinchillas.

From the very first day the keeper has taken on obligations that require regularity and punctuality. Whether animals are fed in the morning and at night or only once daily, it is essential that this is done at about the same time each day. Anyone who believes that animals do not know when they are getting fresh food will soon recognize that chinchillas have a rather precise sense of time, even without a watch! Possibly such punctuality is unnecessary and pedantic, but it certainly can not do any harm either to the keeper or to his animals.

Before we go into the details of breeding and mating, the genital organs of chinchillas and the actual reproductive process must be discussed.

Externally there are only minor differences between the genital organs of male and female chinchillas, since both sexes have genital papillae. In males, the papilla is somewhat larger and longer than in the female, and it contains the penis. The penis is used for the purposes of urination and reproduction, while the papilla in females is only used to urinate. The vagina in females is totally closed except during estrus, and most of the time it can not even be seen. It is located directly behind the papilla and in front of the anus. When a female is in estrus, a perpendicular reddish opening becomes visible. The vagina is normally about 30 mm deep and is subdivided into two sections from the uterine opening onward. In females that have not yet mated and those that have given birth but are not in estrus, a "plug" is formed in the vagina that closes it off. When estrus occurs, the plug is ejected and the female can conceive. This plug looks like a small sac with an opening large enough to accommodate a match. The ovaries are located close to the kidneys, toward the head of the animal from the uterine horns. When ovulation occurs the eggs migrate through the two uterine horns and become attached there when fertilized. In pregnant females that are close to term, the fetus can be felt by gently palpating the animal.

The male's testicles are of an ellipsoid shape and barely 20 mm long. In adult males they can usually be felt from the outside. The penis is supported by a club-shaped baculum, a thin bone. The glandular secretions from male and female genitals coagulate rapidly after mating has occurred to form a vaginal plug in mated females, which should more correctly be called a copulatory or fertilization plug. Its purpose is to prevent the sperm fluid from leaking from the vagina. It is ejected by the female a few hours after copulation. It has a waxy or gelatin-like appearance. It must not be confused with the sac-like estrous plug that is ejected at the onset of estrus.

Let us assume now that the animals have adapted to each other and get along well. There is little else to do other than wait. Estrus in females is not tied to a particular season, and therefore litters can occur throughout the year. Still, most matings (copulation) take place during the cold season. They start in December and reach their peak during January or February, which seems to be a sign that these animals from the Southern Hemisphere have retained the behavioral traits inherited from their ancestors. With a gestation period of a bit over a quarter of a year, most litters are born during the months of March, April, and May. In a large facility it is also not uncommon to get litters during the month of June. Any female not pregnant by then can conceive next only at the end of the year. Copulation is rarely observed from August through November, since chinchillas are less active during that time because the northern summer corresponds to the southern winter. A precise rule can not be established for the mating cycle because matings as well as litters may occur throughout the entire year.

The interval between successive estrus cycles is apparently 28 to 35 days, but individual deviations exist. The opened, reddish vaginal slit is the clearest sign that a female is in heat. The vagina remains open for three or four days and the female can conceive only during this period.

The onset of the first estrus is subject to considerable variations. Depending upon the diet, physical condition, genetic makeup, and glandular functions, a female could have her first estrus already at the age of three months, while others may take up to three years. In these greatly prolonged cases one would expect some abnormal development to have taken place. In order to determine whether a female is in heat, it is picked up at the base of the tail and slight pressure is exerted on the genital papilla. If a perpendicular opening does not become visible, that animal is not in heat.

How often a female comes into estrus depends on various circumstances, but primarily upon its health. General restlessness, pacing or jumping back and forth, frequent scratching of the ground, and obvious swelling of the external genital organs (which may also be blood stained) are all signs of a female being in estrus. In males near females in estrus the testes will become swollen, though they are otherwise barely visible at best the rest of the year. The males tend to obviously court the females and pursue them, but the actual copulation is rarely seen; this occurs in darkness in these crepuscular and nocturnal animals.

The onset of "heat" is not an assurance that ovulation (expulsion of an egg from the ovarian follicle) has actually occurred.

One of the most frequently debated points in chinchilla breeder circles is when to mate chinchillas for the first time. John D. W. Clarke, author of *Modern Chinchilla Farming* (1961), advises against mating chinchillas before they are eight months old. He supports his arguments with the observation that the animals are still growing vigorously at from four to eight months of age. Therefore, it would be wrong to mate females at an age of six months because a developing embryo would place an excessive strain on the development of the female as well as on the fetus. A female should be at least nine months old, preferably even older, before it is mated.

There is much debate among experienced breeders on this point. Some are of the opinion that it is better to mate females at an age of six months because it is easier for these animals at that age to adjust to the selected male, so there is hardly any fighting. Even older, stronger bucks are usually not aggressive with young females. Consequently, the females conceive early and will have their first litter before they are one year old. But such early mated females should not be permitted to conceive again until their young are fully weaned, especially when their litters are larger than two young. Some difficulties will have to be expected if there is a larger age difference between male and female.

Relatively high juvenile mortalities occur in litters that are born from January to April, but there is substantially higher resistance in litters born from May on, so that losses drop to about 10%. The losses during the summer months are notably smaller. This has given rise to a conclusion among American breeders that it does not pay to get litters early in the year. Instead, one should attempt to have the females conceive in late January or February so that the litters would come in May. June litters are also desirable. Experience has shown that once the weather has turned warmer, even aggressive bucks tend to lose interest in females.

There are certain visible signs so that the chinchilla breeder can calculate with some certainty when a litter is due. If he finds tufts of hair while cleaning the cage or when he is just feeding the animals in the morning, he should note the date on the cage card. Then he must be on the look-out daily for the estrous plug, a wax-like structure of 2.5 to 3 cm length that looks like shriveled up rubber, is filled with a pungent slime, and has an opening at the larger end. This plug is ejected from the vagina when a female goes into heat. This, together with the tufts of hair, is an important sign for the breeder that copulation has occurred. Whether it was successful will become apparent within three months. When the copulation plug is found in a fresh condition, it must also be noted on the cage card. This plug is easily overlooked since it can fall through the bottom wire and then dry up. The biological importance of the plug is still unknown. Of course, it can also happen that a female becomes pregnant without there ever having been any signs of copulation. In such a case the breeder will have to expect the litter to come more or less as a surprise. An experienced American chinchilla breeder comments on this: "It is of course helpful to find the copulating plug, but this rarely ever happens. A mere 10% of our litters come from females where we have the copulating plug. This then leaves 90% where we had to determine the pregnancy by other means."

This involves several methods. The safest procedure is to weigh the females once a month. If there is a weight gain during the preceding four or eight weeks, the female can be presumed to be pregnant. Here it should be noted that for this procedure to place as little stress as possible on the animals, they must be hand-tame.

Regular weighing also can be a good indicator for the condition of the animals, so it is particularly recommended for those hobbyists who have just started out with chinchillas. A graph representing weight and day weighed can give important clues about the health and condition of an animal. Since this procedure requires little effort it is also advisable to weigh all bucks at regular intervals of eight to ten· days, preferably before feeding. This provides information as to whether the males are getting the correct amount of grain food, and it can also be used as an indicator of health.

In order to ascertain the physical condition of an animal, it is held by its tail and then rested on the forearm. Gentle feeling along the backbone of the animal down to the base of the tail quickly reveals the differences between a well-nourished animal and one that has had an inadequate diet. Since only the grain fed has an elevated calorie content, one can use this to correct the condition of the animal by adjusting the food rations accordingly. Hay, even if given in large amounts, will not "fatten up" the animals as would grain, particularly corn, sunflower seeds, and linseed.

Weighing females also shows whether they have conceived. Any weight gain is small during the first six weeks, but after that it accelerates rapidly, showing a steep curve, until just prior to birth. Weigh the female twice a month after the first six weeks. It should be noted here that it is easy to be misled by an overfed chinchilla and expect progeny when there is not going to be any.

The observed weights should be recorded on regular graphing paper and the individual observations then connected with a line. Such a curve will vary from one animal to the next, as well as between females that give birth to a single young and those with more than one young. Comparing a number of such diagrams from different animals can provide important information on the adequacy of the diet and the amount of food fed.

As is common practice with other mammals, even with white mice or golden hamsters, gentle palpating can reveal whether a female is pregnant and how far along the pregnancy is, but this requires experience. Very experienced breeders can even tell whether a litter is going to consist of one or more than one young. It must be stressed here that a pregnant chinchilla female must be treated gently and must never be chased around its cage.

It is generally assumed that the normal gestation period for *Chinchilla lanigera* is about 111 days, but the literature also lists 108 days. Numerous reports also indicate that the gestation period can be in excess of 111 days. Apparently, variations in gestation periods between different females can be expected. The gestation period for *Chinchilla chinchilla boliviana* is about 125 to 128 days.

Females will not copulate on the day they are giving birth. Generally the buck is rejected on that day and the next one, but copulations are known to occur on the second and especially on the third day after parturition. So far it is not known whether ovulation occurs before or after copulation.

The fetus develops relatively slowly during the gestation period until the last third of the term. Then it begins to grow surprisingly fast. From that point on, females show a substantial weight gain.

Another procedure to determine whether a female is pregnant is to examine the mammary glands. These being to swell up considerably about two months after a successful copulation, so that the teats become clearly erect. This condition also shows whether a particular female is pregnant for the first time or whether there have been previous litters. In the former the teats are larger and more swollen than in the latter type of female.

Since parturition takes place almost exclusively during the hours of darkness, the breeder will rarely have the opportunity to watch this event. Just as in other mammals, actual parturition is preceded by labor, during which the female appears to be in obvious physical discomfort and emits cries of pain. But under normal conditions it does not take long for the first young to appear, and it is gently pulled out by the female herself. If the litter is of two or more young, the entire birth process takes longer and places an enormous physical stress on the female almost to the point of exhaustion. The entire littering process has not been completed until the afterbirth has been ejected and has been eaten by the female. If by any chance this is being observed, the female must never be prevented from eating her own afterbirth, which would disturb the natural process of this event.

As mentioned by Egon Moesslacher, chinchilla females that have just given birth must not be given a sand bath on that same day. This is essentially a precautionary measure to prevent any infections from contaminated sand particles.

In most instances chinchilla females can handle the entire birth process without any outside help. Immediately upon parturition the female eats the afterbirth and licks her young dry. For the first few hours the young remain under their mother or father, who will keep them warm. Occasionally there can be problems during the littering process, most notably if a pup is relatively large or the female has insufficient muscle strength to achieve normal parturition. If the amniotic fluid has already drained off and the fetus has not appeared after two or three hours, a veterinarian can inject a hypophysis extract that may facilitate the birth process by causing increased uterine contractions. If this fails, the only alternative is a Cesarian section, which of course must be done by a veterinarian.

It is important, especially during the last few weeks of the pregnancy, to pay special attention to the diet. In particular, pregnant females need sufficient calcium, phosphorus, and protein so that the fetus develops normally and the female has an adequate milk supply. Nursing females have the greatest need for a proper and sufficient diet toward the end of the nursing period, particularly since they often have no real opportunity to physically recover because they conceive again shortly after having given birth. In general, pregnant and nursing females do not require a special diet as long as the diet is varied and has the correct nutritional value, especially the supply of minerals. Many breeders tend to overfeed during that period, which may lead to digestive problems, especially if the roughage level is not kept up at the same time.

The first day after the litter has been dropped the breeder must make sure that the young are getting sufficient milk. This is done by palpating their abdomens and observing them closely. If their little stomachs are properly filled, one can assume that all is well. Fighting among the young is a suspicious sign and may be indicative of an inadequate milk supply from the nursing female. If this occurs, supplemental feeding should be instituted without delay.

If there is fighting among the young and they seem obviously hungry, the teats of the female must be checked to see whether they have been injured by the sharp teeth of the young. If this indeed has happened it is advisable to treat any bite wounds with penicillin ointment similar to one used for the treatment of eye infections.

So far there is no documented evidence that it is possible to stimulate milk production with suitable injections, although this seems to be quite a realistic possibility. This, of course, falls within the area of veterinary responsibility.

Under normal conditions the young in each litter are born at intervals from a few minutes to one or two hours. Presumably the placenta (afterbirth) contains certain hormones that are needed by the female, because it is always eaten after parturition has been completed. During the littering process it can happen that the female inadvertently injures one of her young, so the entire litter should be examined shortly after birth and treated if necessary. Various antiseptic ointments and antibiotics have proved to be very effective.

If a litter contains more than two young, it is advisable that every two hours during the first two days the two stronger young are removed from the female for one and a half to two hours so that the weaker pups can drink without being pushed away by the stronger pups. Then all the young are placed together again with their mother for the same length of time. This procedure facilitates a relatively equal sharing among all young of the first milk or colostrum, which contains essential immunity substances for the young. In a strict sense this is not really a milk but instead is a fat- and carbohydrate-rich solution that precedes the actual milk flow. Allegedly colostrum facilitates discharge of the first feces from the intestinal tract of the young. In view of the heat requirements for newborn chinchillas, it is very important that those young that are temporarily removed are maintained in such a way that they can not catch a cold. From the third day onward all the young can remain with their mother.

Young chinchillas are born fully developed: they have fully functional eyes and a complete furry coat just as

Young chinchillas are alert and curious. Remember, they are born with developed teeth and can bite.

do guinea pigs, but unlike many other rodents such as mice and rats and also unlike true rabbits (hares have fully developed young). Newborn mammals in this highly developed condition are referred to as being "precocious." Immediately after they are born, the young chinchillas crawl underneath their mother, who keeps them warm and licks them dry. Their instinct makes them search for the female's teats. This then can lead to fighting (biting) among the young, which can also damage the female. I do not think it is a good idea to file down the teeth of young chinchillas with sandpaper, because these injuries are generally only superficial and will heal quickly. Healing can be further enhanced with an odorless antiseptic ointment.

Some young chinchillas will start taking solid food as early as five days after birth, but of course only in minute amounts. It is important to start monitoring their droppings. Initially these may be somewhat soft and so go unnoticed, since the parents tend to keep the nest box clean. Healthy and well-developed young may appear outside the nest box after the first 24 hours. However, nest boxes are today of such a design that the young have to be somewhat older before they can overcome the height between the bottom of the nest box and the opening above.

In order not to weaken nursing females unnecessarily, the young should be weaned at an age of 35 to 40 days and then raised in a separate rearing cage.

The table shows guidelines for the weight development in chinchillas during their first year:

Age	Highest weight(g)	Lowest weight(g)	Average weight(g)
at birth	57	35	44
at 1 month	200	85	145
2 months	326	255	255
3 months	425	290	340
4 months	489	312	399
5 months	525	340	438
6 months	650	369	485
7 months	780	397	522
8 months	708	397	531
9 months	680	397	548
10 months	758	397	562
11 months	850	397	586
12 months	720	397	556

There have been repeated successful attempts in the United States to artificially inseminate chinchilla females, but this requires specialized technology, equipment, and experience. When correctly utilized and professionally implemented, this opens up the potential to systematically mate particular animals and thus achieve a breeding success that would be unattainable otherwise or at best could only be achieved through years of selective breeding. Of course, artificial insemination can also bring certain disadvantages. For instance, if sperm from a buck of unknown genetic quality is used to fertilize valuable females, the progeny may reveal undesirable characteristics. Unless there are mitigating circumstances, an inexperienced breeder should not experiment with this and it should always be left to a veterinarian. For that reason there are no specific details given here about how to collect sperm from chinchilla bucks. I am under the impression that artificial insemination of chinchillas is a rather delicate, difficult, and uncertain process that is not yet suitable for commercial chinchilla breeding farms.

Sometimes prize-winning stud bucks are offered for sale. Such animals can be very useful to improve the overall quality of animals in a particular facility. Of course, animals like that are always relatively expensive, and before such bucks are purchased the vendor should be asked to show some of the previous progeny of that particular buck. Even then there is no guarantee of a total breeding success since that buck can also pass on undesirable traits. Whether a breeder wants to take such a risk or not depends very much on the circumstances and can really be decided only on a case-by-case basis. It has to be kept in mind that it can also happen that a buck that has not been a prize winner produces very attractive progeny. Therefore, it is best to expect from both male and female parents desirable and undesirable traits in the offspring.

Pairing young animals or placing them in polygamous breeding groups is not difficult at all, but it is recommended that all animals should be at least eight months old.

A breeder is not likely to encounter any difficulties

with pairs that are well adjusted, but problems can occur when a single fully-grown buck or female is paired off with new partners. This quite often reveals that the views of chinchillas are sometimes different from those of their owners. In other words, just as there is love or affection at first sight, the opposite can also occur, jeopardizing the intended man-made bond. Since a situation can arise where a particular partner may have to be replaced, this problem must be discussed.

The female must *always* be placed into the cage of a single buck, and NOT the other way around (except in polygamous breeding setups, of course). Females are sometimes rather aggressive, and they are clearly the stronger sex among chinchillas. When a female is placed into the male's cage she immediately detects the strange scent of the male and so becomes uneasy and unsure. On the other hand, when a male is placed into a cage with a female, he would be immediately attacked as an intruder.

If a breeder wants to be very cautious, he places the female not simply into the cage of the male, but instead into a mating cage. This is an all-wire cage of about 30 x 20 x 30 cm and sufficiently large to accommodate an animal for several hours. As soon as this cage (with the female inside) is placed into the male's cage, the male will come over to investigate and to sniff at it. It is best to observe this without being seen by the animals. The first encounter will quickly reveal the attitude of the two animals toward each other. If there is immediate aggression it is best to remove the female and return her to her own cage, but often the initial aggression fades away to make room for friendly, mutual licking when the buck notices he has a potential mate. His behavior is, without doubt, quite unequivocal. A shy male will not dare to approach the mating cage directly, and he will vocalize to show his displeasure or even his fear, but that too is only temporary. Opening the mating cage and letting the female out depends on the behavior of both animals. If it appears as if both animals are getting along with each other an attempt can be made, but the breeder is strongly advised against keeping the pair together overnight after the animals have only been together for a few hours, because this can result in an unpleasant surprise. It has happened more than once that an attractive male was found bitten to death in the cage the next morning. Even if the buck is only severely injured it is usually enough for him to lose any further interest in mating with other females. Consequently, it is best to proceed slowly and separate the pair again in order to avoid any danger.

A female comes into estrus for the first time at an age of five months. She becomes restless, and if a young buck is in the cage with her, she will court him. In order to prevent such a young female conceiving, she should be transferred to another cage. Years of experience have shown that it is better to mate a female at an age of about eight to nine months. This also applies to young males which also show early mating tendencies while they are still in their growth period.

Usually the vagina, which is located between the anus and the urethral papilla and which is still closed by a horny piece of tissue in young females, opens unaided at estrus, but in some females it may become necessary to soften this tissue with an inert fatty ointment. Thereafter, during periods of estrus, the vagina opens at intervals of 28-34 days. It is then when the buck attempts to mate with the female, which is now in heat. This occurs during the hours of darkness and is preceded by wild chases and some fighting. The following morning one can find the copulatory plug on the cage floor. This of course does not mean that the female has actually conceived; to find out whether a female is pregnant the breeder has to wait another 28-34 days to see if there is another heat cycle. The buck can mate with a female about two days after she has produced a litter. There is some disagreement among breeders whether a female should be separated from the buck after she has littered or whether mating should be permitted again right away.

Precautions must be taken to prevent the young from entering the cage of another female in a polygamous breeding setup via the tunnel used by the male. This other female would, without doubt, kill the young chinchillas.

Practical experiences have shown that getting bucks and females to adjust and adapt to each other can be greatly facilitated and be less dangerous when a particular female's sand bath is also placed in the cage of the buck to which she is to be mated. The male then picks up the scent of the female intended for him and he in turn marks that sand bath with his own scent from his anal sac.

To be on the safe side, it is advisable to keep a flight box in the cage of a newly formed pair to give refuge to one of the animals and prevent one from being injured by the other. In spite of this precautionary measure it is important that prolonged chases are avoided because the pursued animal — usually the male — may get an almost incurable inferiority complex.

There are exceptional chinchillas that will not respond to the procedures described above. If these are females that have desirable breeding qualities and are in excellent pelt condition, it may be worthwhile to put extra effort into their mating. Even though a beginning chinchilla hobbyist may never have to face this problem, it is important enough to be discussed here. As a fundamental observation it must be noted here that there are experienced breeders who are of the opinion that a suitable and compatible buck can be found for even the most difficult and aggressive female. Others have experienced completely hopeless cases. For animals like this it may be worthwhile trying a rubber collar or a muzzle, especially when the female is in heat and one does not wish to miss the period suitable for copulation. With some patience and access to suitably large back-up stock there should be ample choice for a suitable mate for any female.

It can happen that a breeder has to pair off a female with a buck she is not familiar with or place a buck with a female he does not know. If these are young animals about six to nine months old, this requires no more efforts than for other young warm-blooded animals. But it is also possible that if a pair had been together for several years and one has died or can no longer be used for breeding, the other animal of the pair may refuse to mate even if a suitable replacement is immediately at hand. It probably makes sense to give the remaining animal a few days alone until it seeks renewed contact and company. The length of time required for this depends upon the personality of the animal and is therefore very much a matter of individual perception.

In the opinion of Houston and Prestwich, noted American breeders, 95% of all cases of placing new males and females together take place without any difficulties if the breeder proceeds correctly. Among chinchillas there are some animals that are less peaceful or are simply aggressive, just as there are among other mammals. In contrast to most other mammals, the chinchilla female tends to be dominant over the male. This is quite normal, but it must not be permitted to go so far that the female rejects every approach by the male with an attack until the male is so intimidated that he does not try to copulate. Since bucks are smaller and weaker than females, the danger is obvious. Chinchilla bucks have to endure a lot and often sit intimidated in a corner after an aggressive encounter, bloodied by the chisel-shaped teeth of the female, which often does not have a scratch on her. Apparently females are allowed to do anything without encountering any retaliation from the bucks. Here it must be said that bucks have died from injuries sustained during encounters with females, and females have simply bitten them to death! Frightened bucks can be a real problem for their owner.

Minor fighting among the animals is no real reason for a beginner to worry. As soon as he has gained some experience he will be able to determine whether the fight is only a brief, temporary encounter or more serious. Some chasing is common prior to copulation.

One reason for a female rejecting any approach from a buck may well be that she has already conceived. Any female late in her pregnancy should be left in peace if the buck has died. Once the litter has been dropped she can then be mated again, though this is nearly always difficult because the female is still caring for her young and consequently is even more aggressive than usual. Added to this is the risk that a new buck may be hostile toward the young due to his natural instincts. Before such a female can be mated she must be taken out of the cage and placed with a new buck. The separation from her litter can only be a short one, an hour or two at most, since the young must be able to nurse and must not get cold, especially during their first few days.

Pregnant females usually do not pose any problems. They should be left alone, regardless of how curious the owner is to find out whether it is going to be a litter of one or two young. Many breeders feel that even the regular weighings are too much stress on pregnant females. Pregnant females seem to be able to endure being held by the tail, but there is the risk of a spontaneous abortion. Although chinchillas can be lifted up easily by placing a hand underneath them and steadying them by grasping the root of the tail, pregnant chinchillas should really only be handled when absolutely necessary.

A difficult question is the littering date. Even if the copulation day has been duly noted by the breeder — which is not always the case — he still does not know the exact littering date. Sometimes a female late in her pregnancy suddenly become restless and even attacks the buck she is living with; this is a sign to watch for. A chinchilla breeder can never have too many eyes and ears! The better he knows his animals and the more he interacts with them, not only with his hands but also with his brain, the more he can be assured of having success with his animals. Caring for chinchillas requires lots of patience, but this will also be rewarded.

Many breeders will mate their females again within two or three days after a litter has been dropped. This may indeed be the norm in wild chinchillas, but experienced breeders believe the females should be given some rest before they are mated again. At the time when pair-breeding was still the common practice for chinchilla production, bucks and females were kept together permanently so that the female could conceive again shortly after a litter had been born. Now there has been a change over to polygamous breeding, and experience has shown that the females do better if they are given a rest period. Moreover, the young develop better and are more adjusted. It may even be that this method facilitates larger average litter sizes.

The Institute for Fur-bearing Animal Research in Trollesminde, Denmark, has done some comparative studies on this subject. These have revealed that the breeding year is being extended when the females are not mated again until after the young have been weaned, that is, seven weeks after the first litter. A further disadvantage arises in that the litters become distributed over the entire year so that the animals have to be skinned at every season of the year.

Loud and unusual noises as well as unfamiliar visitors should be kept away from a chinchilla breeding facility. Apart from the ever-present risk of disease transmission, it is important to avoid anything that could disturb the animals.

Some breeders place sawdust or wood shavings on the bottom of the nest box, while others may use oat straw or hay. The latter seems advisable during the cold season just before a female is ready to drop her litter, but this is not absolutely essential because females have never been observed to carry straw or hay into their nest boxes. Even a low-wattage incandescent light bulb in a metal can attached underneath the cage bottom is not really required. The light from this bulb must, of course, never penetrate into the nest box. If a litter is expected during the cold season, it may be advisable to provide some supplementary heat. The greatest danger for newborn chinchillas as long as they are still wet is the cold. Usually a female will warm her young and lick them dry, so a heat lamp is really superfluous. When the entrance to the nest box is sufficiently high above the nest box floor so that the young can not get out for the first eight to ten days, then there is hardly any danger of the young animals catching a cold.

American breeders generally remove the sand bath a few days prior to the anticipated littering or no longer give the female unlimited access to it. It is sufficient for the animals to use it once for about half an hour daily. The reason for this is to protect the young from dust, but I do not believe that this is so critical. After all, the animals usually know better than their keeper what is good for them and what is not.

A certain sign of imminent birth is when a pregnant female becomes very inactive, shows a reluctance to move about, refuses to come out to feed, and drives off a formerly compatible buck. Substantial changes in abdominal profile and a steeply increasing weight curve toward the end of the gestation period are further signs, as is the previously closed vagina that becomes very taut, shows a bluish coloration, or starts to open up.

Although the majority of chinchilla litters are born at night or during the early morning hours, there are exceptions. Females that have had prior normal births should not be disturbed by frequently checking the nest box; they will give birth to their young without any human help, correctly bite through the umbilical cord of the young, and will eat the afterbirth. With first litters there is often a certain nervousness, not only among the females concerned, but also among their keepers. Anyone lacking sufficient experience is best advised to leave the animal alone instead of clumsily interfering and possibly spoiling everything. Even domesticated animals that have been exposed to extensive human contact usually go into hiding to give birth. This applies even more so to chinchillas. In fact, it can happen that a female that has been disturbed and has become fearful simply kills her young. Excessive care can do more harm than good.

It must also be mentioned here that cannibalism does occur among chinchillas. This phenomenon, whereby females eat their young shortly after parturition, is also known in many other animals such as captive foxes and minks as well as among cats, dogs, mice, rats, and guinea pigs. There is no complete explanation for this. Instead, it is often assumed that the animals concerned have been disturbed or have become frightened in some way or the young were stillborn or severely injured by the female's teeth during birth. It is not my intention to scare away beginning chinchilla hobbyists or breeders. After all, cannibalism is rare and does not occur very often. Since there is no known remedy against cannibalism, individual chinchillas that engage in this practice must be eliminated from further breeding. If a female has been pregnant repeatedly and has always eaten her young, she must not be used for further breeding. It need not be stressed that observations like this must be recorded on the cage or nest box card.

Chinchillas have functional eyes from birth, but it can happen that the eye lids are encrusted with mucus and are initially closed. Since chinchilla females tend to lick their progeny thoroughly, this problem usually resolves itself. If the eyes are still not fully open after about two days, the keeper can provide some gentle aid by applying lukewarm camomille tea with a ball of cotton wool or by using a few drops of zinc solution available from drug stores.

That is also an opportune time to check the sexes of the young, which must also be recorded. However, before this is done the hands must be thoroughly scrubbed with soap and water. Since the gential organs are poorly developed in young animals, it may be initially somewhat difficult to determine whether they are females or bucks, but practice makes perfect. There actually is no real hurry to sex the animals since they will remain with their mothers for at least another six weeks and up to 12 weeks. Only then will they have to be transferred into their own rearing cages.

According to reports in American trade journals, lack of milk is not particularly uncommon among chinchilla females; this seems to apply especially to Lanigera. The cause for this can vary. In the majority of cases it seems to probably be due to an incorrect diet. If there is a suspicion that a female that has littered a few hours earlier can not feed its young, this must be investigated. An examination can quickly reveal if the female's teats are inflamed, be it because the milk can not get out or because the young with their small but sharp teeth have injured the mother in their eagerness to feed. Inflamed or swollen teats can be gently massaged with an inert ointment or with very small amounts of butter or lard. The animal should be held on her back by someone else while the breeder applies the medication. Within 24 hours the female must be able to nurse her young regularly or the young must be removed. The first litters from young females usually consist of only one or two young; later this may increase to three or four, and in exceptional circumstances even to six or eight. The latter number is absolutely the maximum, and it should not be taken as a blessing. In this respect chinchillas can indeed produce surprises. For instance, Dr. C. J. Call from Idaho had a female that did not produce any young for two years and in fact apparently never became pregnant. Then within the following two years it produced 24 young. The litters consisted of one to five young, with a total of 12 males and 12 females.

Although chinchilla females have six teats, not all of them are supplied with milk. There is some discussion within breeder circles about the number of teats supplied with milk. Apparently there are deviations from the norm in chinchillas, just as there are in other mammals. When milk flows into only one or two teats it means that in a litter with more than one or two young there is a real problem. If the keeper does not attend to this promptly, nature will take over: the stronger animals push their weaker siblings away from the milk source and will grow larger and better while the weaker ones remain behind or even die.

Since chinchillas are valuable animals, the breeder usually will attempt to pull the weaker animals through with supplementary feeding. If it just so happens that there is another female around that has recently lost her young or if a female with only one young is available to become a foster mother for an additional young, the problem is easily solved. However, to accomplish this without a hitch requires a little deception as a precautionary measure. Before the young is given to its foster mother, a highly aromatic oil such as peppermint or clove oil is rubbed around the mouth and nose of both the foster mother and the young she is expected to accept and nurse. This prevents the female from using her sense of smell so she does not notice that she is rearing another young. After a few hours the female will have adapted to the foster child, and from then on she will treat it as her own. Under more normal circumstances, a female chinchilla will attack and kill any young — other than her own — that enters her cage, thus the necessity for caution.

It is relatively easy to persuade female guinea pigs to accept and rear orphaned chinchillas. The female guinea pig can even keep one or two of her own young, since there is usually enough milk for all. The chinchilla young should be about the same age as the guinea pig young, however.

If there is no foster mother available for orphaned chinchillas, they will have to be reared artificially. Bottle-rearing has been done many times quite successfully, yet we have to keep in mind that there is no complete substitute for chinchilla milk, especially since not all its components are known at this stage. American breeders mix evaporated canned milk with an equal volume of camomille tea; initially they give more tea than milk. A sterilized (boiled) pipette with a rubber suction bulb (or an eyedropper) is used to administer this solution. The animal to be fed is held in the left hand with its head between the thumb and index finger, and the solution is given drop by drop directly into the mouth. When doing this, special attention must be paid to make sure that the animal actually swallows and nothing enters its nostrils, because that could quickly lead to suffocation. This requires a steady hand. Initially such hand-feeding may be a bit difficult, but the animals will quickly recognize that this milk is good for them. If the pipette is made of thin glass, the chinchilla's sharp teeth could crack the glass and splinters could injure the animal. Even though this procedure has been used many times with good success, I rather recommend the use of less dangerous rubber nipples as used for doll bottles or pet nursers (available at your pet shop). I have used these on a young mink and managed to rear the animal quite well.

The artificial milk must be lukewarm. At first it is given in minute dosages only and at short intervals so that there is ample time for the liquid to find its way into the stomach. When the suckling — it weighs only 50 to 60 g during the first few days — has had enough, it can be seen from its behavior. Beyond that, you can also feel how the belly is being filled. There must never be any force when milk is given. If by accident some milk gets into the nostrils, the animal will sneeze and eject the liquid. The pup should then be given some time to recover and, if need be, it can be held up by its hind legs or tail so that the liquid can more easily run out of the nasal passages. Initially, the mixture should contain one part milk and two parts water or camomille tea; later it is given at a ratio of 1:1.

Feeding punctuality as described for adult chinchillas applies even more critically to nursing young. According to American practice they should be fed four times daily on warm milk at fixed times early in the morning, at noon, in late afternoon, and at night before bedtime. Giving only three feedings a day may also be sufficient. The larger the animal, the more milk it requires. In addition, the animals should be given some hay and grain right from the start, since they are able to gnaw and feed on some solid food from about one week of age on. Growing chinchillas should be given as much food as they will eat as long as they are not yet fully grown.

Young chinchillas must be closely monitored so that they do not catch cold or have digestive problems. Diarrhea has been successfully treated with a pectin preparation, but prevention is always better than a cure.

Chinchilla litters consisting of three young are not particularly common, and larger ones are even rarer. Even with three young it can happen that the milk supply of a female is not adequate, and consequently the weakest young will remain behind in its development. But there are also females or even entire bloodlines with a fertility higher than normal, where there is a definite tendency — as in some strains of sheep — toward twin and triplet litters. It is, of course, also possible that such an increase in fertility can be interpreted as a manifestation of domestication, just as can the increase in number of mutations. When a breeder obtains an average litter size of two from a large number of chinchillas, he has indeed an above-average fertility among his animals.

When a new breeding colony is being established one should basically expect a 100% increase in number of animals (doubling every year). One's thinking should not be influenced by the fact that chinchilla females can produce up to three litters a year or — expressed more conservatively — five litters in two years. With three litters a year a chinchilla female is under considerable physical and physiological pressure. Therefore, it is advisable to breed for only two litters a year, especially from high-quality females. At that level a female can breed for several years without sustaining any impairment to its reproductive capability.

Practical experience has shown that a breeder can expect an average litter size of about 3.25 young per female per year. Here it has to be remembered that even under the most attentive and scrupulous care it is hardly possible to rear all young from all litters. Moreover, it is an established fact that a certain percentage of breeding females do not conceive and/or the does do not carry the litter to full term. Normally one calculates a loss of 12% or more of the young up to weaning age.

While it was common practice during the infancy of chinchilla breeding to keep the animals in pairs, this has now changed to polygamous breeding groups for economic reasons: it requires less work and lower food requirements. There still are few pedigree bloodlines being maintained, so one would have to expect the occurrence of undesirable characteristics in the progeny that will result in culling. This requires a thorough knowledge of genetics as applied to chinchilla breeding.

What constitutes a manageable breeding facility in terms of size is not clearly discernible from reports by American breeders. Many are satisfied with 200 to 500 animals, which can easily be looked after by two people without any additional help. Assuming that 400 of these animals are females, such an operation would produce an equal or somewhat higher number of pelts per year, which is insufficient as an economically viable operation.

American breeding farms with 1000, 2000, and 5000 animals are not all uncommon. At this time there are no operations in Europe larger than 2000 animals. The largest breeding operation discussed in Willis D. Parker's *Modern Chinchilla Farming* was Rusty's Chinchilla Farm, Anza, California, with a stock of 7800 animals and the facilities to build it up to 20,000 animals.

The American veterinarian Dr. L. R. White has had particularly favorable results from his arrangement of eight enclosures. They are set up as four each, one on top of the other. In between is the enclosure for the

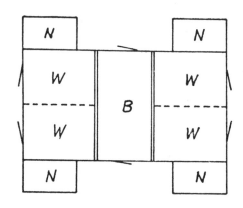

Plan of a cage intended for polygamous mating. Compartment B for the buck; W, compartments for females; and N, nest boxes.

buck, equipped with two bottoms. He has access to the females via a ramp. At each level there are accommodations for two bucks, which must never be permitted to get into direct physical contact, but visual contact is allowed so they can stimulate each other and the females. This type of enclosure construction appears sensible and effective. As an example of the operational efficiency of this sort of polygamous or colonial breeding group, it should be mentioned here that Dr. White obtained in the course of one year 82 young from a single buck.

Another polygamous enclosure, also for a buck and four females, from an American firm is based on a somewhat different construction design. Each of the three cages is 61 x 91 x 48 cm. The bottoms are made of asbestos cement. The doors are as wide and high as the entire front and are equipped with food and water containers that can be filled from outside the cage. This enclosure sits on a table that is 27 cm high and has rubber wheels. This American type of construction keeps the buck and females apart by means of a double gate. The animals become acquainted with each other through this gate, and after a while it is removed so that the animals can then move about freely in the cage.

Other types of enclosure construction are described in professional journals.

This then brings us to a topic that is as equally important and far-reaching as artificial insemination: the quality of breeding stock. Apart from the fact that it is every breeder's aim and objective to constantly improve pelt quality, he is equally determined to produce breeding stock that is as uniform as possible. Both are requirements from the furrier and the fur trade, which are willing to pay more for assortments (matching skins) the more attractive and uniform they are and the more there are. Therefore, it is of paramount importance from a production point of view to use mainly bucks of superior quality for polygamous breeding; otherwise any genetic deficiency has a rather large-scale effect and will recur in the progeny for a long period of time. This is the main reason why bucks that pass on their quality genetically to their progeny often fetch such enormous prices, especially if they are Grand Champions. This also applies to females, but in chinchillas the buck is considered "half the herd." Therefore, it is sometimes advisable to obtain a single high-quality buck, possibly a prize-winning champion, if he can be used to improve breeding quality.

Various reports in the literature indicate that chinchillas in their natural habitat live in small herds or family groups. Invariably an older male is the lead or dominant, just as in other free-roaming animals, such as monkeys. Apart from a lead male, the group consists of several females with their young at various ages. Once the male progeny become sexually mature, fighting erupts between them and the herd's lead male, and the young males usually are driven out of the herd. If, however, the lead male loses such a fight, it is then replaced by the younger male. This natural process is being utilized by some breeders in colonial breeding, where the females do not need a neck collar.

This type of chinchilla maintenance, in which there is allegedly no fur biting, has gained some support in breeders' circles. A detailed, illustrated report about colony maintenance by Lothar Auerbach has been published in *Chinchilla Post* (8/1967) under the title "Experiences with colony breeding." This article carefully evaluates the advantages and disadvantages of this type of chinchilla maintenance. However, colony breeding has not gained general acceptance in Europe or the United States. This gives rise to the question whether this type of maintenance, which corresponds largely to normal conditions, conforms to normal hygienic requirements in the long term. In fox and mink production, colony breeding had to be given up due to the gradual contamination of the natural soil. From a hygienic point of view, a cage bottom is acceptable only if it is not being infected, i.e., a wire bottom with or without bedding.

In the interest of an orderly breeding program it is important to identify the young as soon as they are weaned and transferred permanently to other cages. At that stage their ears are still too small to tattoo, so it is sufficient to mark their tail with a harmless dye (please check manufacturer's recommendations/specifications on Magic Markers and similar products). Similarly, portions of the tail hair can be clipped for ID purposes, but hair will regrow and dye will wear off. From the sixth month onward all chinchillas should be given ear identification tattoos. This can only be done if both ears are undamaged. When the animals fight it can happen (though rarely) that the ears are damaged, which may render the ID marks illegible. In such a case, the damaged ear is to be entered as an identification mark.

Tattooing is done by an electrical device. A thin needle moves rapidly back and forth inside a cartridge, causing tiny holes in the skin that are subsequently rubbed with a special ink. As far as I know, German breeders use only those tattooing machines that have interchangeable characters. These machines and the required characters are sometimes available on loan from chinchilla clubs and associations, since it is not an economical investment for small facilities to purchase their own. Apparently chinchillas experience only very minor pain during the actual tattooing; most of their resistance is due to the fact that they are being restrained. The tattoo identification mark serves to identify the animal, from which facility it comes, its year of birth, and the sequential number of its birth within the progeny from a particular year.

It would indeed be desirable that internationally used rules be introduced. According to these, the left ear is marked with the facility/farm identification mark (letter combination made up of the first letter of the breeder's name or stud/breeding farm designation). The right ear has a letter signifying the year of birth and the litter number or registration number.

ID letters for respective years are used as follows in Germany: A = 1954, B = 1955, C = 1956, D = 1957, E = 1958, F = 1959, H = 1960, J = 1961, K = 1962, L = 1963, M = 1964, N = 1965, P = 1966, R = 1967, S = 1968, T = 1969, V = 1970, X = 1971, Z = 1972, A = 1973, B = 1974, C = 1975, D = 1976, etc.

The letters G, I, O, Q, U, W, and Y have been omitted. The Canadian system commenced at a later year, also starting with "A". In the United States the letter system used to identify the year was started back in 1935.

The letters and numbers of a tattoo are supposed to convey the origin (facility or breeding farm) of an animal, when it was born, and its individual identification number. Regrettably, this system is not necessarily totally reliable unless the specific origin of an animal is known. In addition, some breeders do not adhere to the international identification rules.

If a newly tattooed animal walks around for a few days with its ears hanging down — until they are fully healed — this is nothing really to worry about. It is far worse if one suddenly notices that there are some mistakes in the codes and letters, because it is extremely difficult to make subsequent corrections.

Superficial tattooing injuries, to a point where a little blood is drawn, are unavoidable. Therefore, it is advisable to have an ample supply of sterile gauze or cotton balls handy.

So far we have discussed primarily the practical aspects of chinchilla care and maintenance, but now we have to turn our attention to the administrative side of things. This does not have to turn into a paper war, but if a beginner takes down a few more details than appear necessary, there is no harm done; this is far better than having to worry about details that were not — but should have been — recorded. Moreover, a small chinchilla breeding facility does not require much paper work, but it should include those records that gain in value and significance as time goes on and as more comprehensive experience is gained.

A cage card must be attached to each cage, fastened in such a way that the animals can not chew on it and so render it illegible. Ideally, the card should have a clear plastic protective cover. It must have the following details: 1) Sex and number of animals; 2) DOB (date of birth); 3) # of litters for females; # of progeny for bucks; 4) Date of copulation; 5) Litter date; 6) Evaluation.

The decisions whether to immunize chinchillas and with which vaccine are best left to an experienced veterinarian. There are now some that have gained considerable knowledge in this area. Their addresses are published in professional journals. Fundamentally one has to distinguish between a prophylactic immunization and an injection against an acute disease. The former initiates the production of specific antibodies, defensive substances that render the body immune for a variable period of time against a particular disease. Chinchilla farms with large stocks must immunize their animals for economic reasons. After all, this relatively minor expense can not be compared to the losses that can be incurred due to an epidemic.

Chinchilla vaccines are manufactured by an American and a German manufacturer. The American product, called "CHIN-VAC," is made by Dr. Keagy. Unfortunately the manufacturer does not indicate the date of manufacture or its expiration date. It can be obtained without a prescription and is not registered with the German Department of Health. A vaccine made especially for European conditions is "CINQUACCIN," manufactured by Behring A.G. in Marburg, the largest manufacturer of vaccines in Europe. This particular vaccine was produced in cooperation with the Institute for Small Animal Breeding in Celle and is available only to veterinarians. It has proven to be effective in many cases. The decision whether an entire stock should be immunized must be made by a veterinarian.

Of course, these preparations are not effective against all infectious diseases of chinchillas, but they do offer an increased security to any breeder who is concerned about the health of his stock. In effect, it is a sort of life insurance for his animals. One of the prerequisites for this to be maximally effective is, of course, that the breeder does everything that is required to maintain his facility clean and hygienic as a prophylactic against possible diseases.

There are a number of systems in use to evaluate/assess the quality and condition of chinchillas. The best known is the International Evaluating System of Willard H. George, which was introduced into Germany by Gerhard Schreiber, Munich. On the other hand, Canada uses an evaluation card that is monitored by the Ministry for Agriculture. There is, in addition, a European Chinchilla Evaluating System that is based on a point score of 100. These and other systems consider visible pelt characteristics and not genetic traits. (The latter are determined by evaluating the pedigree certificate.) Different evaluation systems are in use in Scandinavia and some other countries.

In order to be independent of variable daylight levels, chinchilla breeding stock is evaluated under an evaluation lamp. This is a stable light source that provides concentrated monochrome light. Since the cost of such a lamp is relatively high, it can really only be considered as an economic investment for large breeding facilities. Evaluating fur-bearing animals is an activity that is influenced by a number of factors. In order to achieve largely unbiased evaluation, various prerequisites have to be met. The person doing the evaluation (assessor) must have the ability to distinguish even the slightest color variation, especially the "faulty" colors such as yellow, brown, and rusty, and to define these correctly. This sort of work must, of course, always be done under completely identical light conditions. Extensive tests and research have revealed that the most suitable light type is the Type L, 20 W/15 Daylight fluorescent light made by Osram.

In spite of every good intention, one could not expect that the results of several judges assessing the qualities of a single animal would be exactly identical. Therefore, it is indeed commendable that experienced chinchilla show judges from West Germany, Holland, Austria, Sweden, Switzerland, and Belgium (regrettably not from France) have joined together to form the Working Party of European Chinchilla Judges. This Working Party has established uniform show rules and guidelines for chinchilla performance shows in consultation with relevant American, British, and Swedish regulations.

The evaluation certificate showing the necessary details for each animal is important to successful breeders. An absolutely indispensable supplement to this is the pedigree certificate, which reveals details about parents, grandparents, and earlier ancestors. The pedigree certificate also lists the tattoos of an animal as well as those of its ancestors, the size of the litters from which it and its ancestors came, all evaluation results, and other relevant remarks. Such a pedigree contains a large amount of information, and for animals with quality ancestry it provides reasonably accurate information about the progeny a breeder can expect. Apart from the actual pedigree, there is a listing showing the buck and/or its ID symbol and details of all matings (ID of females, litter dates, and the number of bucks and females obtained from each litter). This rounds off the breeding background for an animal and offers an opportunity to combine its characteristics with those of an equal or superior partner with the objective to produce pelts of greatest beauty.

On the other hand, one must not over-estimate the value of these papers: apart from the fact that occasionally they are of doubtful reliability — especially for imported chinchillas — proof of high pelt returns is increasing in significance. In fact, this is already a requirement for most breeders. Anyone wanting to sell breeding stock must be able to show proof of prices he was paid for pelts from his facility.

Although all details are properly recorded, an efficiently operated chinchilla breeding farm also includes the maintenance of a diary. Here we note what has happened, whether there have been any litters or losses, the occurrence of diseases, the arrival of new animals and the sale of animals, feeding details, temperature and humidity readings; in short, anything that is of interest to the breeder and that may conceivably be of interest at some later date. Such a diary can be kept in a standard appointment calendar. Also of considerable importance is the breeding book, which is also an inventory book. A ring binder with a separate sheet for each animal is perfectly adequate. The breeding book contians a record of every animal born or acquired from an outside source, the sex of this animal, cage number and identification number, litters born to this animal, and when it died or was skinned. This facilitates a quick, effortless review of matings and their results, as well as any losses and details about animals skinned. For the sake of completion it is suggested here that those breeders who immunize their animals regularly must also maintain a vaccination record.

Maintaining a pelt book is of greatest importance. Here we record the ID marks of those animals skinned and the monetary return from each skin. In addition, we include remarks about the condition, appearance, and color of the skin, and we note whether these have been emergency cullings or were part of the regular skinning program. Apart from the breeding book, the pelt book is the very basis of a successful breeding operation, because it clearly reveals information about its economic viability. The sale of live animals for breeding purposes is now considered to be really little more than welcome extra income.

For the sake of correctness it must be pointed out here that the breeder must also maintain — for tax purposes — a detailed record of all of his income and expenses associated with his chinchilla breeding operation.

When Chinchillas Are Sick

Generally speaking, chinchillas do not get sick easily in captivity. In any event, it should not be more difficult to keep chinchillas in good health than it is to keep rabbits, guinea pigs, and similar animals healthy. I am sure most experienced breeders share this opinion, even though it may be with certain reservations. Keeping chinchillas healthy includes giving proper nutrition and care, as well as providing adequately ventilated but draft-free housing.

Nevertheless, one must also be ready to deal with a chinchilla or two that may become sick. It is not really possible to anticipate this sort of thing, but much can be done to prevent the occurrence (and spreading) of a disease. A successful animal keeper or chinchilla breeder will immediately notice — without making any special efforts — whether his chinchillas are in good condition and doing well, or whether an animal has diarrhea, suffers from constipation, or has some other disorder. In time, observing the animals will become second nature to the beginner, and this habit must never be lost. A few days, sometimes only hours, can be decisive for the life of an animal. If, for instance, a case of diarrhea or constipation is permitted to go on untreated, it is possible that all help will come too late. The beginner can be assured that if he takes care of his animals correctly he can sleep soundly. Yet, during the feeding periods he must be totally alert, and then it is better to observe a bit more than not enough. Chinchillas when frightened may cast off tufts of fur. Therefore, it is advisable to treat chinchillas gently when they are handled.

The reader is cautioned against believing that chinchillas never get sick. It is important to acquire the proper knowledge before a problem occurs. Of course, a veterinary handbook does not replace the veterinarian. After all, treating a sick animal requires far more thorough knowledge than can be obtained merely by reading a book. Even a veterinarian who has no experience with chinchillas will in some instances be facing real problems with these animals. For that reason it is only intended here to provide a general overview about the more relevant disease problems in chinchillas. In addition, there may be some suggestions offered here based on practical experience.

Minor (superficial) bite and scratch wounds can be treated easily with a disinfectant solution or with a wound powder or ointment available from drug stores. If healing does not progress properly a veterinarian must be consulted.

Infectious diseases, often of unknown origin, can occur. Apart from the obvious requirement to immediately isolate an affected animal in a separate room (quarantine/treatment room), there is little the breeder can do other than to thoroughly wash the cage, food dishes, and utensils with an effective disinfectant solution. Even more effective is the flame of a blow torch, which penetrates into all cracks, crevices, and corners.

Diarrhea as a consequence of wet green food can be treated with medical charcoal or similar preparations available from drug stores.

Constipation is often somewhat more difficult to treat. The breeder can try increasing the green food or can add a very mild laxative to the drinking water; camomille tea can also be tried. Karlsbad salt (a pinch added to the drinking water) is known to provide effective relief.

Unfortunately, beginners have a tendency to overfeed their animals and are then surprised if there is no progeny. The best diet is ample amounts of hay together with modest amounts of grain. Anyone seeking advice on how to look after chinchillas can also turn to a more experienced colleague or to the supplier of his animals. Failing this, you should contact a veterinarian experienced with small mammals, preferably with chinchillas. It is a good practice to have all emergency addresses and telephone numbers handy before a disease problem arises. Under no circumstances should the breeder attempt to do any surgery or other complicated treatment himself. Antibiotics are possibly effective against some infections, but the decision to use them should be left to a veterinarian. Sulfonamides should also be considered in such cases.

Infectious diseases include those caused by fungi. These involve primarily the digestive system, causing diarrhea, and arise from feeding moldy hay. Apparently chinchillas are not very resistant to this sort of problem. In this case, prevention is the best defense. Anyone who makes it a habit to smell the hay before it is given to the animals can easily avoid diseases caused by fungi; quality hay always smells pleasant, while moldy hay has a distinctive odor. Old leftover hay must always be removed from the cage and breeding room before fresh hay is given. If one is certain that moldy hay is the cause of lack of interest in food with or without the occurrence of diarrhea, this must be mentioned to the attending veterinarian. He will then attempt to treat the animal with sulfonamides and charcoal or pectin preparations. In any event, a prolonged case of diarrhea — especially if more than one animal is involved — requires a bacteriological examination of the droppings, which is usually done by veterinary pathology laboratories. A suitable medication can only be found if a specific pathogen is implicated and identified.

During periods of humid and warm weather, especially in late summer, chinchillas are sometimes infected by a fungal skin disease. This disease-causing fungus is related to the fungus that causes athlete's foot. If a fungal infection is detected before it has spread over the entire body, then the scab-like patches can be treated by dabbing them with concentrated alcohol.

With fungal infections, and in fact with any infection, regardless of its origin, it is absolutely essential that all affected cages and the breeding room be thoroughly disinfected. The best and most effective way of doing this is by carefully using a blow torch on appropriate surfaces and veterinarian-recommended disinfectants on other surfaces. A blow torch has to be used cautiously in view of the potential fire danger; breeding operations are known to have gone up in smoke because of the careless use of blow torches.

Fungi can cause other diseases, such as eye infections. Secondary fungal infections following mechanical injuries are often difficult to cure. A very effective and inexpensive medication against fungal diseases is Ortozid (Captan 50). It is essentially a plant fungicide that is available from tree nurseries, where it is used to treat fungal pathogens affecting fruit trees and vines. Practical experience has shown that small amounts of Ortozid can be mixed into the bathing sand without causing any harm. This should be done as soon as there is the slightest suspicion of fungal pathogens. A typical symptom includes the loss of hair, first around the snout and then later around the eyes, the bare skin patches becoming red and inflamed.

Finally, I have to mention a behavioral phenomenon that is not exactly uncommon: fur biting. Hardly any other topic has been discussed in the trade press as extensively as this one. Apparently it is due to a number of different causes. For instance, it is supposed to be caused by the diet, a nutritional deficiency similar to that of feather biting among birds. In these cases a change in the diet might eliminate this sort of behavior and condition. There may be other causes for this behavioral phenomenon, but these have not yet been clearly determined. If one notices fur-biting in other facilities, it is best not to purchase any animals and to leave the premises as quickly as possible.

Fur biting (also called fur breaking) can have various causes, including ectoparasites, nutritional deficiencies, vitamin deficiencies, and probably unknown causes. Willis D. Parker is convinced that pelt damage is rarely due to fur biting but instead is due to an infestation by *Trichophyton mentagrophytes*, a fungus pathogen.

Other factors that could cause fur biting may be improper nutrition, damp breeding rooms, insufficient ventilation, deficiencies, and (especially) excessive noise. Crepuscular and nocturnal animals such as chinchillas must have peace and quiet during the day and

Unless recommended by your veterinarian never spray your chinchillas with any insecticide. If a parasitic problem exists the veterinarian will recommend a specific treatment.

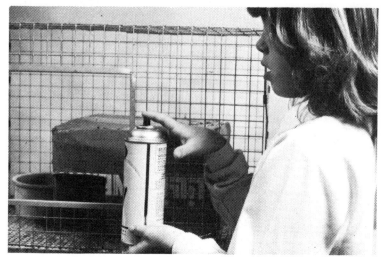

they also need it at night. If these animals are placed in a room that is constantly exposed to street traffic and other noises, it should not surprise when they do not look well and have a poor breeding record. Still, there are always those who think they know better.

In serious cases fur biting can lead to the death of the affected animals, but even in less serious cases the fur is still being adversely affected. Moreover, fur biting can easily be transmitted to other animals in the same enclosure. Between 5 and 6% of all North American chinchillas are affected by fur biting, according to J. W. Houston and J. P. Prestwich. There are also stocks that are affected up to 90%.

It is obvious that damage caused to pelts can hardly be due to simple gnawing or biting, especially when it usually starts at the whiskers, around the head, and along the back, all places where a chinchilla, when kept by itself, can not reach. It is imperative that treatment be left to a veterinarian.

Mites and other pest organisms can occur in or be introduced into a chinchilla operation, but these are not difficult to eliminate with suitable agents — see your veterinarian.

The American chinchilla literature often refers to a phenomenon called "slobbers." It manifests itself by saliva flow or "drooling" and is due to unsatisfactory dental occlusion (teeth/jaw closure) because of teeth having broken off or an uneven growth of the gnawing teeth. This impedes food intake and the animals lose condition. If this is noticed in time — and there is no reason not to if the animals are constantly being monitored — such dental impairment must be corrected. This, however, is very much a matter for a veterinarian. As soon as it is noticed that an animal is not feeding properly, it should be examined and if need be — taken to a veterinarian. Dental anomalies must always be treated by a

181

veterinarian. This must NEVER be a self-help project.

This discussion of chinchilla diseases is not intended to discourage anybody or to lead to complacency. It can not replace the veterinarian. Instead, it provides only suggestions and hints without unnecessarily worrying the beginner. It must also be appreciated by the reader that an attempt is made here to give some sort of overview of possible chinchilla diseases which does not mean that all of them have to occur.

Eye infections can occur in chinchillas. There are eye drops available from your veterinarian. If an animal has some mechanically caused injury, a sulfonamide preparation is often quite effective.

An incorrect diet often leads to constipation. Sometimes all that is required to improve this condition is extra green food, but the breeder has to make sure that this is indeed taken by the affected animal. The intestines of a chinchilla are about 10 to 12 times as long as the total body length. Gently palpating and massaging the abdomen, together with giving green food, can provide relief. The later this condition is recognized, the more difficult it becomes to correct, because of the enormous length of the intestine.

Diarrhea is more quickly recognized. It is usually the result of too much green food, especially in spring, when the animals have been fed apples or vegetables for a prolonged period of time. When diarrhea occurs it is best to stop feeding any green food and fruit. Because of loss of fluids, the animal gets thirsty, a fact that is used by giving the animal a pectin preparation diluted with boiled water. This home remedy can only provide relief from diarrhea when too much green food has been given. If, however, diarrhea persists for a few days it may well be due to an infection. The treatment of such an infection depends upon a bacteriological examination (by a veterinarian) of the droppings.

Newly acquired chinchillas can display various disorders that often affect kidney and liver function as a result of dietary and climatic changes. Even kidney stones are mentioned in the literature.

Colic (flatulence) can also occur when wet green food is given. Other causes are lack of exercise because the cages are too small or overcrowded and the presence of an infection. A preparation that contains *Lactobacillus acidophilus* can bring relief for colic and even cure this disease. Sulfonamides and streptomycin are also recommended as treatments. Colic in horses sometimes responds favorably to a prolonged period of heavy exercise.

Nursing females sometimes suffer from an inflammation of the teats or mammary glands due to premature lactation or because of injuries caused by the sharp teeth of aggressively nursing young. If only one of the teats is affected, the breeder can try warm camomille compresses several times daily and gently apply colorless (inert) petroleum jelly or lanolin ointment. In more severe cases the young will have to be removed from their mother and the treatment left to a veterinarian. Lactating disorders usually occur shortly after parturition or during the first three weeks after the birth of a litter.

Chinchillas are rarely exposed to tuberculosis and this disease rarely occurs. Animals with obvious respiratory difficulties (coughing, labored breathing) must be removed immediately and kept in isolation. The former cage must then be thoroughly disinfected. On the other hand, pseudotuberculosis is not exactly rare.

Abscesses can develop as secondary infections due to mechanical injuries. They usually will burst without any help, and they should then be treated with a suitable liquid or ointment medication. In some cases it may be necessary to remove the surrounding hair, cut open an abscess, and squeeze it out. Cysts are similar to abscesses but they are formed by endoparasites, such as tapeworms, that are introduced via the feed (hay). Opening abscesses can be done by the breeder, but cysts should be treated by a veterinarian in order to avoid infections.

Active animals that tend to jump a lot may incur a bone fracture, particularly when they become entangled in wire mesh. Accidents like this always necessitate a visit to the veterinarian. Healing is usually rapid once a proper splint has been applied.

There are two types of convulsions that can occur in chinchillas, and sometimes both of these can occur simultaneously so that they are barely distinguishable from each other. One of these is due to a calcium deficiency, the other because of a lack of vitamin B. The former manifests itself in muscle spasms that sometimes are so severe that the affected animal appears totally distorted — the hind legs are extended, the tail is bent over, the face muscles are distorted so the teeth are displaced, and the ears are laid back against the head. It can happen that such an animal loses control over its voluntary muscle system. These convulsions are most likely to happen just before the feeding time. Such feeding convulsions can be counteracted by feeding animals with such afflictions first. If the convulsion is extremely severe and lasts for a long time, relief can be provided by quickly administering an intramuscular injection of calcium gluconate. If at all possible, this injection should be avoided because it can lead to calcium deposits in the muscles once the injected calcium combines with phosphorus in the tissue and blood of the animal. Sometimes the calcium is absorbed by the body system, but it can also happen that swellings form at the site of the injection. As a prophylactic measure against calcium deficiency, one gives calcium gluconate, calcium lactate, dicalcium phosphate, or bone meal, as well as vitamin

D, together with the food. A temporary calcium deficiency can easily be remedied when suitable measures are initiated before any serious damage is done. Harmful afteraffects rarely occur.

Vitamin deficiency convulsions manifest themselves frequently before feeding. The symptoms are severe trembling, and the animal is unable to control muscle movement; it leans against a cage wall and drags the hind legs as if it is unable to walk. This type of convulsion is due to a thiamine deficiency which affects not only tissue, but also the nervous system. Consequently, a prolonged convulsion of this type can lead to paralysis, especially in the legs, and serious cases can lead to the death of the animal.

A countermeasure can be a quick intramuscular injection of thiamine or the entire B complex in order to provide rapid relief. Regrettably, neuritis resulting from the injection often does not subside very quickly, even though the symptoms may have disappeared after the first treatment. A complete treatment requires massive doses of vitamin B complex over a period of two or three months. This must include an adjustment of the diet so that after the treatment has been completed the former deficiency has been eliminated. The preparation can be administered via food or drinking water. In all of these cases a veterinarian must be consulted without delay, as it should be he who will then decide how to treat the sick animal.

Since time immemorial it has been common practice to castrate those male animals that were not required for breeding purposes, be it to improve their meat qualities or their appearance. This applies to castrated roosters as well as to turkey cocks because their meat is more tender. Rams and boars are castrated for the same reason, while a castrated tom cat is more peaceful and is more attractive.

Therefore, it seems to be relevant to consider castrating chinchilla bucks in order to obtain a denser pelt. This has been done on farm-bred mink in the Soviet Union. Those animals had a lower food consumption because they were apparently better able to utilize the food, and they also seem to have had more attractive pelts than non-castrated males in a control group. Another advantage is that several males can be kept together in the same enclosure, which saves time and work; they are more peaceful and get along better with each other. Among non-castrated mink males there would soon be fighting and losses would occur.

This should also hold true for chinchilla bucks, which have a tendency to be rather aggressive. Although there are no relevant practical experiences on record, it can be assumed that castrated bucks will be compatible in a community enclosure.

It must be pointed out though, that castrating chinchilla bucks does pose some problems for anatomical reasons. In contrast to the minks and cats, the testes in chinchilla bucks are located in the abdominal cavity. This means that castrating requires professionally administered general anesthesia because this is a major surgical procedure. It must be done by a veterinarian under totally sterile conditions.

This raises the question of whether it is economically feasible to get chinchilla bucks sterilized by a veterinarian for a fee that could possibly exceed the anticipated monetary return. Yet this idea should not necessarily be abandoned. One should consider the possibility of whether castrating might not provide a reasonable return by getting a larger number of bucks castrated by a veterinarian at an agreed fixed fee. At this stage this is merely a suggestion since there are apparently no practical experiences yet in this area.

Obtaining Chinchilla Pelts

Until a chinchilla matures and is considered to be an adult, its fur undergoes three developmental stages during the first year of the animal's life. At birth the animal has what is known as the baby coat, which gives little indication of its eventual level of quality. This changes into the juvenile coat at an age of three to four months. This provides the breeder with the first indication about pelt quality that can be anticipated, so a decision can then be made whether to retain the animal or whether it should be skinned. Chinchillas in good condition will change their coat once more at an age of seven to eight months and are then considered to be fully mature adults.

All relevant details and observations about condition and pelt development must be recorded by the breeder, because with increasing stock it is impossible to rely on memory alone. From year to year such records will become more valuable for the operation of a chinchilla farm. They reveal what animals should be mated in order to enhance, suppress, or eliminate particular genetic characteristics.

Somewhere along the line the time will come where the breeder has to put down some of the animals that he has raised. Since there are animal lovers who are unable to do this, this point must be carefully considered before money is invested in a chinchilla breeding facility.

Most other rodents and similar animals are killed by holding them up by their hind legs and firmly hitting them against the back of the head; rabbits and nutria are often killed by this method. This kills swiftly and effectively. Once the animal is dead it should hang head-down for some time to make sure that blood does not contaminate the fur, which would seriously affect the price for the pelt. Other breeders prefer to put their animals down by using the exhaust gases from a gasoline engine. For that purpose the animals are placed in an air-tight container that is hooked up to the exhaust pipe. This procedure is commonly used to put down minks. A similar method involves the use of chloroform. Some time ago breeders changed over to cervical dislocation ("neck breaking") as a more rapid killing method, provided one is experienced with this technique, but not everyone is inclined to do this sort of thing. Finally, mention must be made of electrocution to kill chinchillas, but the breeder is strongly advised against using this method.

Practical experience has shown that chinchillas should only be killed by using chloroform (preferably in an air-tight, large glass container) or cervical dislocation.

With chinchillas, as with all fur-bearing animals, there is a time when the pelt is at its peak of condition ("mature"), when it should be harvested in order to obtain the best price. It is the unique advantage of captive breeding that the breeder can wait for just the right moment, while pelts obtained in the wild are of necessity often not mature yet or are already past their peak condition.

In both species of chinchillas, prime pelt maturity occurs from December through March. In most young born prior to 1 June the pelt does not mature before the following winter. Pelt maturity is ascertained by blowing against the back of the animal, from the neck back along the backbone, in such a way that the hair parts. If a pelt is mature the skin at the base of the fur is white or grayish white; an immature pelt has pink or blue skin.

Depending upon the physical condition of the animal, its nutrition, environmental factors, and other more or less influential factors, pelt maturity in chinchillas occurs for the first time at an age of between eight and ten months. Young chinchillas born between the end of the year and the following spring will therefore gain pelt maturity during next fall or at the onset of winter. Just as the majority of litters are dropped in spring and fall (although litters can occur throughout the year), pelt maturity generally occurs in summer or winter. As one would expect, animals that reach pelt maturity during the winter months have a denser coat. When pelt maturity occurs during warmer periods of the year, the coat is somewhat less dense, which, however, is not significant. Although females can be mated after six months, this should preferably be done somewhat later, unless they are very strong and well-developed. Young bucks that are to be used for breeding must be at least nine months old. Both sexes continue to grow until they are about 15 months old.

Pelt maturity can be speeded up artificially as reported in an article the German breeder Rold Haupt, who had conducted experiments in this area. He writes (*Chinchilla Post*, 2/1975) that this pelt maturity can be artificially induced when the daylight period is increased with artificial lighting followed by complete darkness in a regimen where the annual light cycle is compressed into about 16 weeks. Uniform temperatures of about 22°C and a relative humidity of about 50% must be maintained throughout. He actually obtained mature pelts in this manner, but he also believed that natural maturity is less expensive to accomplish. He did not notice an improvement in pelt density.

At this time there is still considerable controversy within breeder circles about the diet of those animals designated for skinning. Some will give ample amounts of food to their animals in the belief that this speeds up hair growth and pelt maturity; others keep these animals on a marginal diet including little or no starchy ingredients but ample amounts of hay. It appears to me that the marginal diet is more appropriate since it corresponds essentially to the winter months, which under normal conditions is also the time for the best pelt maturity.

Chinchillas designated for skinning are often kept on a bedding of wood shavings in order to prevent discoloring of the pelt, particularly of the abdominal region. This bedding is changed frequently. Other breeders consider bedding to be unnecessary and maintain their animals on normal wire bottoms.

In due course the beginning chinchilla breeder will gain experience and learn to recognize mature chinchilla pelts. It is of paramount importance to avoid under any circumstances the occurrence of animals that show even the slightest hint of a yellow or brownish tinge. With this even the most attractive pelts become essentially worthless since the trade refuses to take them. A yellow discoloration can also be caused by incorrect maintenance (dirty cages) and other external factors. Old fur apparel from before the war almost always shows a yellowish discoloration that even the best of care can not eliminate since it is due to age.

Until a few years ago the pelt harvest was of lesser importance because trading in live chinchillas was far more lucrative. But the objective of chinchilla breeding is to make a profit from the sale of quality pelts. Breeders in North America and throughout many European countries are now realizing this.

For show purposes and for evaluating and sorting skins, there are now four color classes that are commonly recognized: medium light; medium dark; dark; and very dark. Dark pelts of suitable quality currently fetch the highest prices but the trade always looks for rarity, and demand is dictated by fashion. The most important objective for a breeder remains *uniformity of skins and their color.*

Which color or color tone is the most attractive is a matter of individual taste. Generally speaking, the medium dark and dark pelts are more impressive due to the contrasting lighter abdominal area. Dark pelts are currently achieving the highest prices, but this is purely a matter of fashion preference which may well change in time.

Whether chinchilla color mutation pelts are to be given any value at all by the fur trade and if so what kind, is a question that may not be answered for years to come. It will certainly take a long time before suitably large assortments of these mutations come onto the market. Beginning breeders are advised against breeding mutation chinchillas unless they have the financial resources, the skill, and a thorough knowledge of gentics. At this stage it is more important that the world market is supplied with high quality, flawless standard pelts in sufficient numbers. The word "standard," by the way, refers to chinchillas of natural gray pelt color.

When this book was published in 1956, there were no chinchilla mutations around yet, but with rapidly increasing breeding activities one would have expected them to occur sooner or later. At that time I recommended to my readers to watch out for deviating colors and for young chinchillas with light or dark patches. I suggested the same thing again in the 2nd, 3rd, and 4th editions, and by and large it still applies to this day. Since then there have been a multitude of mutations. Although the first snow-white chinchillas were traded at fantastic prices, it has become clear that the fur trade is not interested in this color.

Apart from white mutations, there are also a number of other established color shades. One recognizes beige, silver, pastel, champagne, and cream, as well as light brown mutations. Lately black velvet, sapphire, and charcoal mutations have been added. In contrast to the majority of these mutations, the black ones are supposed to be of excellent pelt quality. The breeder of these blacks, Bob Gunning from Davenport, Washington, needed more than ten years to stabilize this mutation. He started out with a female that had a black head and mated her repeatedly with the darkest bucks available. His black velvet chinchillas were a sensation at shows. When one considers the vast multitude of mutations among minks, one can well imagine that the development in chinchilla breeding may follow similar paths.

In order to improve pelt quality, mutation animals may well be useful to the experienced breeder, but whether mutations will ever become a commercial success is still an unanswered question. Although sufficient assortments of beige and black velvets are already available, the response from the fur trade has so far been only lukewarm.

Clarity of color is the determining factor for the condition of a pelt — the overall impression and the color of the band, the veil, and the undercoat. Beyond that, pelt sorters pay particular attention to density, texture, density of veil, and hair elasticity. When a live animal is being evaluated, its size, body form, neck fur, evenness of the band, and hair length, as well as presence of guard hairs, play an important role. The abdominal fur should be pure white and not extend too far up the sides.

For the time being, however, the budding chinchilla breeder does not have to worry about how to select those animals with the most attractive pelts, although I encourage him to keep his eyes open. For mating the animals it is absolutely imperative to know which animals are best suited for each other in terms of their pelt characteristics. Whether one should attempt to selectively breed for chinchillas with the darkest "blue" possible or give preference to the light-colored silver-gray is impossible to say in advance; it all depends on the preference of unpredictable fashion trends. Presumably, the pelts most keenly sought after are invariably those that are the rarest. Anyway, that is the way it is on the international fur market.

Every breeder must know how to skin a chinchilla. When an animal dies he can use it to practice skinning and thus learn how this is done. (It goes without saying that afterward the carcass must be sent as quickly as possible to a suitably qualified veterinarian or veterinary research laboratory for an autopsy in order to determine the cause of death of such an animal.) Breeders who for some reason or other are unable to skin their own animals can take them to a central skinning facility. It is advisable that the breeder accompanies his animals to see and learn how they are skinned. Such skins are identified with a seal so that they can not be mistaken for those of other breeders.

In the previous edition of this book I had written: "A prerequisite for skinning chinchillas is that the body is not completely cooled off and rigor mortis has not yet set in." Prof. Dr. Kraft, in his book *Diseases of Chinchillas*, also states: "We recommend that skinning is done immediately after killing the animal. For one thing, it is more easily done on a warm carcass, and beyond that it prevents the skin from being contaminated with substances that could possibly cause pelt damage." In contrast to this, a standard text, *Chinchilla ABC* (published by Roland, Munich) states: "The dead body should be permitted to cool off for at least two hours before it is skinned." This indicates that even experts do not always share the same opinion on fundamental points.

It is not that skinning a chinchilla is difficult or requires a lot of effort; all it takes is a certain training and experience that can only be gained with time, and everyone has to start some time.

Initially chinchilla skins came onto the market as "bags" (one-piece skins not slit ventrally), but now it is common practice to cut along the abdominal midline and spread the skin for drying. Handling the pelts requires a lot of skill so that the skin is not stretched too much and becomes distorted.

The following equipment is required:
1) A strong pair of scissors, a furrier's knife, or a scalpel with replaceable blade.
2) A skinning board of about 35 x 50 x 55, or 45 x 60 cm and about 15 mm thick.
3) 10 furrier's pinning needles per skin, but NOT thumb tacks or regular needles, which are useless for this purpose.
4) Fine hardwood sawdust that is very absorbent; bathing sand or corn meal can also be used.
5) Four metal spring clips that are secured at the four corners of the skinning board with ring screws.
6) A brush made of natural bristles, not too stiff; nylon bristles are too stiff.
7) An umbrella shaft with groove, blunt at the top.
8) Tension boards, 15 cm wide by 50 cm length.
9) A skin preparation agent to prevent decay.
10) Sealing pliers and pelt seals to identify pelts.

When pulling the skin of the carcass it is important that hands and fingers always remain dry and fat free, which is best done by rubbing the hands in sawdust. This is the best material to soak up fat. In order to avoid contaminating the pelt with fat, it must only be handled at the edges. When cutting, only the outer skin must be penetrated, not the flesh underneath, so that the pelt is not ruined by blood stains.

This brings us to the actual skinning. The tools and equipment are spread out on a sufficiently large table. The animal is turned on its back with the head pointing upward. Then all four legs are clamped down so that the body is attached securely to the skinning board.

Pulling of the skin is done in the following manner:

1) The sex organ of the animal is held up between left index finger and thumb. The knife is inserted just above it and an incision is made in the direction of the head. Great care has to be taken so that only a small vertical incision is made in the skin.

2) Now the umbrella rod (blunt side first) is inserted into the opening and pushed forward cautiously between pelt and body skin in the direction of the head. The rod must not penetrate into the abdominal cavity. When the rod touches the chin it is pushed strongly through the bottom lip or a small cut is made in the lip and the rod is pulled out through the lip.

3) Then the umbrella rod is pushed again between pelt and body skin at the first incision with the left hand, lifting it up slightly so the groove is at the top, and the pelt is cut open toward the lower lip. The blade moves along the groove as a guide.

4) A cut is made toward both hind legs. For that purpose an incision is made between joint and foot on each hind leg and the umbrella rod is inserted until it reappears at the original incision. This is repeated on the other hind leg.

5) The pelt cut open in this manner is pulled away from the body with the left thumb and index finger, but only for a couple of centimeters on either side of the cut so that the pelt is not unduly stretched. In order to keep body fat and blood off the pelt, care has to be taken that ample amounts of sawdust or bathing sand are spread over the skin.

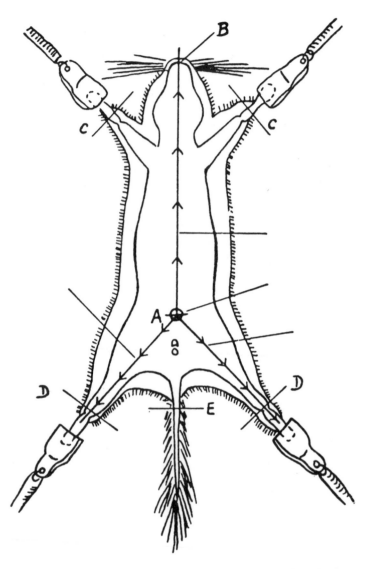

A diagrammatic illustration of the process of skinning a chinchilla showing the location and direction of the incisions.

6) Pulling the pelt away from around the head, one must proceed very cautiously so that it is not damaged. For that reason the nostrils are widened with incisions made with a pair of scissors or a scalpel. Then the head is held firmly and the pelt is removed slowly away from the skull with small incisions up to the eyes. There must be ample use of sawdust to avoid blood and fat stains.

7) Now the front legs are released from the spring clips and the bone is severed just below the joint so that only small stumps remain inside the pelt. The ears are cut off from the outside of the pelt, severing the cartilage. It is imperative that the basal cartilage be removed because the furrier has no need for the ears and the pelt can be damaged when the ears start to decay.

8) Then the head skin is cut loose from around the eyes, which must not be injured in this procedure. This must be done very gently so as not to tear the pelt. The entire pelt can now be pulled off from the head and front legs.

9) It is recommended that you release the body from the pelt, and not the pelt from the body, to assure that virtually no flesh or skin remnants remain attached to the skin.

10) The entire process is concluded by cutting the tail in such a way that the pelt is pulled over the tail bone and is severed about 2 cm away from the body; the furrier has no use for the tail.

Cleaning, spreading, and shaping of the pelt follow skinning. First of all, the pelt is placed leather side up on the spreading board and every attempt is made to remove all fat and flesh remnants in order to avoid subsequent damage due to decay, which could render the pelt worthless. After that it must be spread and tightened on the board in order to give the pelt the correct shape;

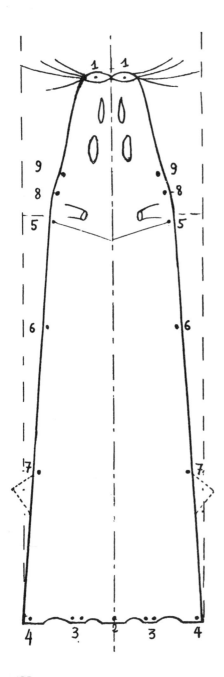

Illustration of a chinchilla pelt fastened on a spreading board. (After G. Schreiber, *Peltzungfibel.*)

this must be done without undue delay. Pelts must be permitted to dry at natural temperature and must not be exposed to artificial heat.

Skinning a chinchilla is a matter of training and experience. As soon as you have skinned and prepared a dozen or so carcasses, you will be familiar enough with the details and will not longer require specific instructions.

Each chinchilla pelt is marked with a seal. These seals can be acquired from fur companies or breeder associations and bear consecutive numbers. Each seal number should be recorded by the breeder in his pelt book before he sends his pelts off to a fur company or a furrier.

After the mounted pelts have been drying at room temperature for about four or five days the pins are removed and the skin is gently brushed out. These raw skins are stored by suspending them from clothes pins. In order to prevent moths, fur beetles, and other insects from depositing their eggs on newly prepared pelts, commercially available chemical insecticides or preserving agents can be purchased. Fur companies refuse shipments that have fur parasites so as not to infest their own pelt stocks. The dried pelts require no further work.

Once a pelt has a slight tear, this often becomes larger very quickly. Pelts become slightly less sensitive after tanning has been completed. Raw pelts should be packed in pairs so that sides with the fur are facing each other. Two such pelts are then wrapped in newspaper and packed in a cardboard carton. If you proceed correctly the result will satisfy the requirements laid down by furriers and preparators. One thing is certain: the individual breeder is best advised not to market his own pelts, because this will only bring him disappointments.

When breeding fur-bearing animals the objective is generally to harvest pelts, but I am firmly convinced that it is indeed feasible the harvest and utilize the hair (or "wool") of chinchillas. The large number of inferior pelts in North America could thus be put to good use, rather than having to burn them.

A simple test that can easily be made is very convincing. If one twists a tuft of hair, as is commonly found in chinchilla cages, one will notice that this hair can easily be twirled into a thread; in other words, chinchilla hair can be spun.

At this stage it may still seem unlikely that chinchillas will become suppliers of a fine animal fiber that could not even be approximated by artificial production methods, but we have to recall that early writers knew that the old Peruvians used to make exquisite and wonderfully warm blankets from spun chinchilla hair. Anyone who deals with this material closely will quickly realize that chinchilla hair has an insulating property hardly matched by any other animal hair, including that of angora wool. Whether one makes knitwear or ladies apparel out of it is a question only to be answered by textile experts.

In fact, according to an illustrated report in the *Chinchilla Post*, the ladies apparel company Feldpausch in Basel and Zurich offered coats made of a material woven from sheep wool and chinchilla hair. This material was characterized by a silky sheen and a so far unknown softness and pliability; despite its fineness it was incredibly solid.

I made an inquiry to the American Museum of Natural History in New York whether they had any knowledge of or even a collection of cloth woven from chinchilla hair. In response to this I was advised by Dr. Junius B. Bird, Curator for South American Archaeology and an internationally recognized authority in this field, that he knew nothing about such material. Apparently the Indians who lived in the Andes had a long tradition with spun material, and they used every conceivable material that could be spun. Without doubt they must have used chinchilla hair when available, but he was not aware of such material. However, he did know of a turban strip from the Nazca Indians that was estimated to have originated in the 10th Century B.C. and which was woven in part from the hair of viscachas (*Lagostomus*). This hair, however, was used only to decorate the ends of the strip, while the remainder of the cloth was made of alpaca wool. The latter was dyed, but not the viscacha hair.

Any hair that can not be spun can still be used for the production of felt articles. As is well known, the felt industry uses the hair of rabbits and hares as raw material. Beaver hair was also used during the early years of this industry, primarily for the manufacture of the most expensive hats for men.

Leipzig and its famous Bruehl were once the world trade center for fur apparel. Not far from there, mainly around Markranstaedt, there were tanning and preparation shops that because of their years of experience were able to prepare chinchilla pelts in just the way required by furriers. These skills may have become forgotten and are therefore lost forever. In the meantime, tanning techniques and tanning chemistry have achieved great advances, so in this respect the required technology is certainly available. There is also supposed to be a procedure whereby pelts are "blended" with sponge and dyes so as to disguise any flaws or mismatches. However, man will never achieve the same beauty as nature, much less exceed nature. The most beautiful pelts are still those that have not been "improved."

Marketing Chinchilla Pelts

Several decades have passed since the last chinchilla pelts — about 4,000 skins — were auctioned off in Leipzig. In the meantime this beautiful fur had almost vanished into oblivion. Here and there we may still see the occasional elderly lady with a chinchilla shawl, collar, or perhaps even a chinchilla coat that must have cost a lot of money even in those early years. Today such garments look worn and have only historical value. Those early skins were exclusively from wild-caught chinchillas. Fur garments made of chinchilla pelts were once highly fashionable, the most elegant apparel a woman could own. Because chinchilla furs have a unique beauty, fashion — once again — will make chinchilla furs what they once were — the most precious fur next to sable.

Due to well-funded persistent advertising, mainly by the National Chinchilla Breeders of America, garments made from chinchilla pelts have once again become a symbol of preciousness and beauty. In fact, they are now more frequently seen in the shops of up-market furriers and at fashion shows. It must be remembered, though, that chinchilla is not and never has been worn during the day. It remains the most exquisite evening fur, because only candlelight or electric light gives it its mysterious glow.

All available literature references, starting with Joseph de Acosta (1591), without exception point to the extraordinary fineness of chinchilla hair. It was described by Ignazio Molina as being "as delicate as the silk spun by garden spiders." This opinion is certainly shared by the author of this book. Yet precise measurements have — as far as I know — never been made.

Even at the risk of destroying a popular illusion among chinchilla breeders, it must be stated that chinchilla hair is not the finest in the world. I have made every effort to check on the accuracy of this widely accepted impression, and I am now in the position to offer a final word on the subject.

In response to a request from me, Mr. Werner von Bergen, Assistant Manager of the Central Research Laboratory operated by the textile company J. P. Stevens & Co., Inc., Garfield, New Jersey, conducted a test on two chinchilla hair samples on 11 May 1961. Mr. von Bergen is considered to be an international authority in the area of textile fibers and has published more than 50 scientific papers on this subject. The laboratory passed on to me the following test results:

Material tested: hair samples from *Chinchilla lanigera* (Velligera) and *Chinchilla chinchilla boliviana* (Brevicaudata), thickness distribution as follows:

Microns*	C. lanigera % of sample falling in micron range	C. c. boliviana % of sample falling in micron range
0-10	3.0	2.0
10.0-12.5	18.0	17.0
12.5-15.0	29.0	32.0
15.0-17.0	31.0	34.0
17.5-20.0	14.0	14.0
Above 20.0	5.0	1.0
Average in microns	15.04	14.88
Standard deviation	3.0	2.5
Deviation from the norm	0.21	0.18
Variation coefficient in %	19.9	16.8

*1 micron = one thousandth millimeter.

Upon Mr. von Bergen's suggestion, I approached Dr. H. E. Froehlich, manager of the Research Institute of the Hutindustrie e.V. Moenchengladbach, who is considered to be an authority in the area of animal hairs. I am indebted to Dr. Froehlich for the following information:

Type of Hair	Fineness in microns
Chinchilla (dorsal)	13.0-14.0
Mink (dorsal)	12.0-12.5
Nutria (dorsal)	10.8-11.2
Beaver (dorsal)	10.5-11.0
Muskrat (dorsal)	about 14.0
Muskrat (abdominal)	about 10.0
Angora rabbit	about 12.0
Winter hare (German) (dorsal)	about 12.5
Fall hare (German) (dorsal)	about 13.0
Wild rabbit (Winter, dorsal)	13.0-14.5
Domesticated rabbits (Winter pelts, depending upon color)	13.5-16.0

Furthermore, Dr. Froehlich informed me, "We believe that the incredible softness of the chinchilla fur is due to the fact that the pelt has practically no guard hairs. An additional factor is probably the layer of scales that is thinner in chinchilla hair than in other fur-bearing animals, which consequently further enhances the softness. Presumably further details about the fine structure of chinchilla hair will come to light from further studies in this area."

Whether one likes it or not, one has to accept the fact that although chinchilla hair is of great fineness, the hair of angora rabbits, muskrats, nutria, mink, and winter hares is clearly finer yet, and only wild and domesticated rabbits have hair that is marginally coarser than that of chinchillas.

Of course, this long overdue correction does not take anything away from the beauty of chinchilla pelts, which remains unexcelled.

The reason for the regular annual increase in chinchilla skin prices in the international fur trade is a sad chapter of human greed and superstition. As reported by early writers, chinchillas were once common well into the coastal regions of Chile. When chinchilla pelts became fashionable in the 1890's, a relentless hunt for their skins was set in motion. In order not to damage the skins, the Indian trappers used snares to catch these animals. Inevitably this also killed many young animals. Due to the low productivity of these animals, their population declined rapidly. Apart from the fact that the skins were relatively well paid for by fur buyers, the Indians also hunted chinchillas because of a superstition: they believed that chinchilla meat was a medicine against tuberculosis, which was rampant among Indian populations at that time.

Consequently, chinchillas were pushed back more and more into inaccessible areas at higher and higher elevations. This was certainly true for *C. lanigera*, which was considered to be a strictly coastal species, as indicated by its Chilean name, Costina. On the other hand, the larger *C. chinchilla* was probably always more of a mountain-dweller.

QUANTITIES AND PRICE MOVEMENTS OF CHINCHILLA PELTS IN LONDON*

Year	Approximate number of pelts	Wholesale price German marks (DM)
1900	300,000	17.–
1901	300,000	20.–
1902	175,000	26.–
1903	150,000	18.–
1904	110,000	25.–
1905	45,000	37.–
1906	45,000	37.–
1907	56,000	36.–
1908	52,000	35.–
1909	24,000	135.–
1910	17,000	135.–
1911	13,500	150.–
1912	21,000	180.–
1913	4,000	150.–
1914	4,000	155.–
from 1914-1919	no details available	225.–

From 1920 onward annually only a few hundred skins to Europe.

*Derived by R. Gloeck from London auction catalogs.

Before World War I, chinchilla pelts were traded mainly in Leipzig, London, and Paris, and also in Buenos Aires and New York. The late Richard Gloeck, fur trader in Leipzig, reported:

"For prepared Chilenas I received 1 to 2.50 Marks for large skins in 1889; between 1890 and 1893 the price varied from 0.75 to 3 Marks. The first 'Reales' appeared on my ledgers in 1894, and they have brought up to 15 Marks each. Turn-over increased significantly during the following years, and prices shot up. My largest turn-over was in 1899, 78,500 skins that brought up to 12.50 Marks each."

Cages made of wood and chicken wire have been found inferior in comparison to modern cages made of metal frame and spot-welded wires.

As reported by the Chilean physician Dr. Juan Grau, Santiago de Chile, the export of chinchilla skins from Chile in 1899 consisted of 435,463 skins. Exports dropped to 247,836 skins in 1905 and to 152,863 by 1910.

Laws to protect chinchillas against their complete extinction were introduced in 1918. Dr. Grau has done much pioneer work in researching and publishing details of the natural history and feeding behavior of the Chilean chinchillas. These details, which are valuable to both breeders and the future trade in chinchilla skins, show how frighteningly fast the number of chinchilla skins declined due to merciless hunting pressures on these animals. Simultaneously, these figures also show how sluggishly the price quotations followed the supply trend, obviously indicating anticipation of an increase in the number of skins available for sale.

Regrettably, there are no details available on the species distribution within the total offering each year. Only Gloeck reveals that more than 300,000 Chilena skins and about 20,000 Reales skins came onto the market in London in 1899. To this we have to add odd lots that were imported directly from South America. Initially these were distributed solely by Felix Faure & Cie, in Le Havre. The owner of this company later became President of France. In response to my inquiry to the Hudson Bay Company in London about details of turn-over and quotations of chinchilla skins around the turn of the century, I was advised that records of these transactions were not available.

According to Brass, the number of Reales, Bolivianos, and Chilenas was about 120,000 skins in 1910. This included about 6,000 Reales skins and an estimated 25,000 Chilena skins. Chile alone exported 80,000 to 100,000 chinchilla pelts at that time. The Reales were selling for around 900 Marks per dozen, 75 Marks each; Boliviano skins about 500 Marks per dozen, 41.70 Marks each; Chilena skins about 300 Marks per dozen, or 25 Marks each. For the year 1925, Brass lists a figure of 2,000 to 3,000 skins of Reales and Bolivianos combined and 6,000 to 8,000 Chilenas skins coming onto the market during the year. At that time Reales and Bolivianos were treated at 8000 to 10,000 Marks per dozen, that is, between 667 and 833 Marks each; Chilenas sold for 2000 to 3000 Marks per dozen, or 167 to 250 Marks each.

A close comparison of these figures reveals that these statistics are rather unreliable, but even if other data are included the overall picture does not become any clearer.

In 1929 Martin Nilsson took a small lot—presumably Boliviano skins from his farm — to London. He told me that he had received an average price of 50.10.0 pounds sterling, or nearly $250 each. The highest price at that time was 60.0.0 pounds sterling, or $300 each. Later he confided in me that the entire lot consisted of only five skins.

If one calculates the skin price based on the number of skins required for coats or similar large fur garments, the unit price goes up to 1400 Marks per skin for Bolivianos. After WW I a German furrier was given an order for a chinchilla coat together with an offer of 125,000 Marks, but this had to be declined because the required number of skins was no longer available at that price.

At the International Fur-bearing Animal Exhibition that took place in Leipzig in 1930, a list was circulated giving the world production of animal skins. Within the context of this chapter, this list may still be of interest today. The listing started with an annual world pelt production figure of 200 million rabbit skins and concluded with the following table:

Silver fox	80,000 skins
Pine marten	75,000 skins
Fur seal	65,000 skins
Lynx	58,000 skins
Leopard	23,000 skins
Blue fox	23,000 skins
Siberian sable	15,000 skins
Chinchilla	500 skins

Skins that have commercial value only in lots can become a considerable disappointment when they are sold individually. This is particularly true for chinchilla skins. It is absolutely essential that they all match in color and quality so that they can be made into uniform fur garments. When chinchilla skins came onto the world market by the thousands, skilled experts would sort them into lots where the skins within each lot would be closely matched. Sometimes the skins would be bundled or sold unassorted. A very similar process takes place with mink skins. On one occasion there were 58 different chinchilla assortments on offer at Leipzig, with a total of many thousands of skins. Although at the beginning the fur trade was no doubt inclined to make certain concessions in regard to purity of assortment, its demands soon increased. After all, uniform assortments are the very basis of the beauty of fur garments. This was evident in the odd fur garments that appeared at various places before the last war.

Valuable supplementary information to this topic comes from a lecture given to a convention of American chinchilla breeders by Frank G. Ashbrook, a well-known American writer on matters relating to fur-bearing animals and an official of the U.S. Fish and Wildlife Service. Listed below are some of the essential points of that lecture:

Around 1890 the better quality chinchilla skins would fetch $13 on the open market. At that time large numbers of skins were still being traded. Statistics maintained by the Customs Department at the Chilean port of Coquimbo in 1905 still show the surprising export of 216,000 chinchilla skins. By 1906 this had dropped to 108,000 skins, in 1907 to 61,000 skins, and to a mere 27,000 skins in 1909. It must be noted that top quality skins could command at that time (1909) around $40 each. The conservation laws that had been passed by various South American countries were essentially never enforced. Prices for top quality chinchilla skins jumped to $50 and then to $150 (a Gold Mark value of easily 200 to 600 Marks). The last available early quotations are from 1930, prior to the devaluation of the dollar, and were $200 or more than 800 Marks each. These prices were even quoted for individual skins when repairs to fur coats required chinchilla pelts at any price. Chinchilla skins not suitable for fur coats were widely used as adornments on hats, evening gowns, or as supplementary material for other fur garments.

Individual skins, regardless of their quality and size, are of little or no value to the furrier, and this is often a disappointment to the inexperienced breeder when he can not find a buyer for these skins. But anyone who knows the market situation would not even attempt to offer individual skins to a furrier. The value of chinchilla pelts does not lie in their density, silkiness, hair length, and size, but instead in the assortment to which they belong. An assortment is a smaller or larger number of pelts that are largely uniform in quality, color, and size. Assortments with a large number of pelts fetch higher prices than smaller assortments, because to assemble a large assortment requires thousands of skins from which to select. Sorting and assembling assortments is a type of work that not only requires experience but also a certain innate talent. Therefore, sorters as specialists in this field are paid very well by fur companies and furriers.

In any event, all this clearly shows that it is in the interest of the chinchilla breeder if his harvest is marketed through a commercial pelt buyer. As an individual he has very little chance of obtaining a reasonable return on the open market unless he operates a very large breeding facility that produces animals of even quality and appearance. Since this is today hardly ever the case, the only realistic way to achieve a reasonable return is to collectively market the skins from small harvests from a number of breeding facilities via a commercial buyer of chinchilla skins. It is generally customary for breeders to send in their chinchilla skins untreated, and the buyer arranges for preparation and tanning and also gets them ready for marketing. This of course also cuts down the overhead for the small breeder.

On 21 June 1954, for the first time in more than half a century, an auction of chinchilla skins was conducted by the New York Auction Company, Inc., in New York on behalf of the National Chinchilla Breeders, Inc. This was the first auction of domestically produced pelts. The breeders' association had been advising its members in advance for many months to prepare their stocks by removing all animals that were unsuitable for further breeding and skinning all excess stock. Since the general public and the fur trade were no longer familiar with chinchilla pelts, the association spent about $100,000 on a publicity campaign to attract the attention of the public and the media. In contrast to expectations, the number of skins taken to auction was surprisingly small: a mere 10,850 skins. Although a substantial number of inferior quality skins had apparently already been removed, those available for the auction still left much to be desired in terms of their quality. The sorters of the New York Auction Company managed to assemble a collection of 529 bundles with 20 pelts each. Only the top ten bundles were of top class; they obtained $101.45 (more than 420 Marks) per pelt. The price was $60 per pelt for the second best ten bundles. The average yield for the auction was $44.20 per pelt. The very best bundle was acquired by the furrier Leo Ritter, New York, at a price of $175, a premium price that was inflated due to the publicity. Finally, by the time the bids went down to $11 per pelt, only about 45% (or 4761 pelts) of the stock available had been sold. At that point the rest of the collection, which consisted predominantly of damaged merchandise and assortments that were below par, was withdrawn.

Various conclusions can be drawn from these figures. First of all, they indicate that only really good pelt quality attracts top prices. Regardless of the number of animals held by breeders, the percentage of top quality pelts is apparently small. Thus the 4761 pelts sold were only of sufficient quality for about 60 shawls and jackets made up of 45 pelts each. The material was totally inadequate for full-length coats, which would have required about 120 chinchilla skins each. Here it must be pointed out that coats require a far larger selection of pelts because, since each pelt is different, obtaining an assortment of matching pelts for an entire coat requires a selection of hundreds of skins. At the turn of the century, when London was still the most important chinchilla market and had an annual turn-over of about 300,000 skins, there were 58 different types of assortments.

At most, 10% of all commercially farmed mink pelts offered at auction are of top quality. The world production of mink pelts in 1975 was estimated to be 16 million skins, and for years before that it was as high as about 25 million skins. In 1975 the world production of chinchilla skins was estimated to be 120,000 skins, of which about 10% would be top quality — 12,000 chinchillas versus 1,6000,000 mink. It must be said that there is still a lot of work as well as financial reward waiting for the genuine breeder.

The action taken by the National Chinchilla Breeders of Canada is exemplary. Upon being admitted to the Association, each breeder must obligate himself, on the basis of a marketing contract, to deliver his entire skin harvest to the Association. The organization alone has the right to decide which skins are suitable for sale and which are not. It can destroy useless pelts — without compensating the breeders — if experienced individuals confirm with their signature the pelt identification marks involved in such disposal action. Private sale of skins is totally prohibited. This indeed is a highly sensible measure, especially with pelts that may be worth something within a particular assortment but would be practically unsellable and worthless as individual skins. In order to prevent open and direct sale of skins by members, the contract stipulates that any proven violation of this rule requires 50% of the proceeds to be paid to the Association! Of course nobody is forced to sign this contract — but a non-members' animals are not evaluated and his skins can not be marketed via the

National Chinchilla Breeders of Canada, NCBC.

One of the most frequent but very understandable questions is: How much does a chinchilla pelt cost? This is very difficult to answer with a few words. Fundamentally, a single pelt, even if it is very beautiful, has only academic value because a furrier can do little with an individual pelt. Such a pelt gains a true value once it becomes part of an assortment, a bundle of skins selected and assembled by experts from thousands of skins. The larger the assortment and the more matching and attractive the skins are, the greater the assortment/bundle value and the greater value per pelt.

Anyone who contemplates breeding chinchillas either to supplement his income or as a profession is of course interested in the financial return of his capital investment. Therefore, it may initially be more relevant to ask: What are the costs involved in producing a chinchilla pelt, and what is the market price that can be expected for it? The unit production cost involved varies from one breeding facility to the next. It is made up of the cost of purchase of the breeding stock, its amortization, expenses incurred for caging, rent, feed, and electricity (heat and lighting), and other general expenses. In addition, there are labor costs. Even as a part-time venture, the breeder must include his time as a cost factor. The costs involved in establishing a chinchilla breeding facility can only be legitimately determined on a case-by-case basis, preferably from one's own experience. In Germany, a recently determined "average" for feeding costs alone was about 15 Marks per animal per year. As you already know, the return per pelt varies tremendously based on quality and the market.

For practical reasons, furriers when selecting chinchilla pelts tend to place emphasis not only on quality, but they also try to buy bundles containing pelts that are as large as possible so fewer pelts are required for particular pieces of fur apparel. Therefore, breeders should also select for size in their breeding program, and smaller animals (such as the Raton type) should be excluded from breeding, even if they meet qualitatively all prerequisites.

In respect to size of skins and other characteristics, there are limits to what a breeder can expect to accomplish. In this context it may be relevent to refer to the experiments by the geneticist Dr. Hubert D. Goodale, U.S. Department of Agriculture. For decades he had been breeding white mice strictly for size, disregarding all other characteristics. At the birth of the 35th generation of white mice he noticed that the average weight of his animals at 60 days of age increased from 25 g to 45 g. However, from that point on he was unable to increase the average weight of his mice further, although he maintained the selective breeding program up to the 49th generation. His stock varied from 100 to 1000 animals for each generation, with an average of 649 mice. A total of 54,535 mice were involved in this experiment, which was certainly one of the largest ever conducted on a mammalian species.

In order to offer at least some relevant figures, the reader's attention is drawn to the sales results of the Chinchilla Pelt Center in 1976. A total of 5517 pelts was sold at a price of 257,805 Marks (DM). In 1975 the Center turned over 3949 pelts for a total of DM 195,660. Pelts from France and West Germany achieved the highest price of DM 150. The averge price of DM 49.30 increased to DM 50.38 in 1975. The largest lots available were 1649 pelts at DM 50 each, 520 pelts at DM 60 each, and 458 pelts at DM 80 each. A price of DM 90 each was paid for 76 pelts, 153 pelts went for DM 100, 12 pelts at DM 120, eight pelts at DM 130, and only six pelts at DM 150 each. More of the top quality pelts could have been sold had they been available, but who would skin his top quality animals to be used for further breeding?

The lowest price of DM 20 each was paid for 453 pelts. Such a low price is, of course, totally unsatisfactory for the breeder, but these were the pelts of inferior color quality or damaged pelts from breeding animals that had died.

The budding breeder is advised to consult with successful breeders and furriers and check professional trade journals for current market information since supply and demand constantly fluctuate. It is also recommended that he visit chinchilla exhibitions and shows as regularly as possible and there constantly compare animals and prices. It is very important to gather as much experience as possible in this field. In time one learns to recognize quality, an ability that is advantageous to have before more money is sunk into a chinchilla breeding facility.

Chinchilla pelts can really only be marketed in two ways: by selling individual pelts privately (this market is generally very small) or giving the pelts to a wholesaler on commission. Individual and unsorted pelts are essentially useless to the fur trade. This is easier to understand when one appreciates the fact that fur apparel *must* be made from matched pelts (sorted into suitable bundles) and specially selected from a minimum of 5000 pelts. Sorting chinchilla pelts requires years of experience and an innate "eye" for quality pelts, just as is required for appraising other skins and live animals. Once again it must be pointed out that the pelts from prize-winning breeding stock do not always fetch correspondingly high prices.

Anyone who does not believe that chinchilla breeding is still totally unknown within large circles of our population can convince himself without great difficulties. It is sufficient to mention this topic in discussions with people on the street, in bars or waiting rooms, or on other occasions, and ask whether anybody knows what chinchillas look like, where they come from, what they feed on, and who is breeding them. One can be assured of a totally inadequate or completely wrong reply. This must not only be food for thought, but one should also come to the conclusion that there is still a vast and hardly explored territory for selling chinchilla breeding stock. One only has to know how to discover it.

Small advertisements can sometimes be very effective, especially when they are placed where they are least expected so they are given a lot of attention. It is well known that advertising can be profitable assuming that it is done properly, although it is expensive. Anyone who offers "information about breeding chinchillas" should have a properly designed prospectus available for distribution. To design such a prospectus — preferably by an advertising specialist — costs money for paper, printing, and, if at all possible, color separations. It is more economical if a number of breeders get together on this or, better yet, an entire club or association, to produce such a leaflet jointly so the individual participants only need to place their rubber stamp imprint or printed name and address on it. This gives the advertising a more professional appeal rather than having to distribute mimeographed sheets that might give the impression that there is not much money to be made from chinchilla breeding. Everyone must clearly understand this.

Advertising is not the only way to find new customers. Anyone confident enough to speak in front of a crowd can give lectures about chinchilla breeding to establish personal contacts and so build a bridge to success. Such lectures must, of course, include slides, which can say more than a thousand words. These can be taken in one's own breeding room, possibly by a skilled amateur photographer. A professional photo-graher may produce better photographs, but he also expects to be paid properly.

Now, how can contacts be established with groups that might be interested in a lecture entitled "Breeding chinchillas for fun and profit" or something similar?

This is simple: Every major city has clubs for breeders of cage and song birds, poultry, dogs, bees, and other similar hobbies. Their addresses usually are easily obtainable. Then a visit is paid to the chairman or president and you tell him something about chinchilla breeding (about which he may not have known anything at all) and offer to give a slide lecture about this topic — free of charge, of course — at the next club meeting. Since you are not viewed as a competitor who wants to poach members, and since meetings are usually not that entertaining, it should not be difficult to set up a lecture date. When listeners at the conclusion of the lecture still have questions, these can be answered on the spot. It may also be advantageous to leave a few multicolored pamphlets behind to keep the topic of chinchilla breeding alive.

But this still does not exhaust all possible ways to promote chinchilla breeding. One should also consider manning a stand at an exhibition or show that features lots of different animals. This has been done in Sweden, where an exhibition has been held under the theme "Recreation with animals," which had wide public interest, particularly since the local media always like to report on public interest events like this and so provide free advertising. This particular show in Sweden had 170 exhibitors with more than 1000 animals, including birds, fishes, rabbits, dogs, and of course, chinchillas. An attractively designed show catalog provided further information as well as the addresses of clubs, associations, and exhibitors.

Man always has had strong and emotional affinities for animals as shown by the visitors crowding into zoological parks. Chinchilla breeders should take advantage of this to promote their aims and objectives. I have attempted here to suggest a few possibilities in this direction, but this does not mean that there are not others possibly even more promising and successful.

The fact that the furrier needs pelt assortments from which he can make fur apparel is sufficient evidence of the need for chinchilla breeders to become organized. The type of success that can be achieved is best seen among the breeders of mutation minks in the United States. Only the infusion of considerable amounts of money enabled these breeders to secure markets for their annually increasing pelt harvests.

But these are not the only reasons for breeders to organize themselves. The main task of a breeder association is to advise and instruct its members on breeding and skinning techniques and on other relevant details about fur-bearing animal production. Such an association also organizes events such as standard (performance) shows and exhibitions for animals and pelts, as well as arranging expert evaluation of breeding stock and enforcing rigid breeding standards. In the past there has been much neglect in this area in virtually all countries where chinchillas are being bred.

An absolutely essential tool to promote quality breeding is performance shows where the best animal material is given awards and certificates of recognition. Additionally, such shows expose successful breeders to a wider audience and promote the cause of chinchilla breeding to the general public. Moreover, animals are traded at such shows, particularly valuable breeding stock, and breeders have an opportunity to compare their breeding stock with that of others. Similar tasks are also carried out by trade journals.

References

Acosta, J. de: *Historia Natural y Moral de los Indios.* Sevilla, 1591.

Albert, F.: "La Chinchilla, *"Anales de la Universidad, Santiago de Chile*, 1900: 913-934.

Ashbrook, F. G.: *Fur Farming for Profit.* New York, 1929.

Bachrach, M.: *Fur.* New York, 1930.

Brass, E.: *Aus dem Reiche der Pelze.* Berlin, 1911.

Brehm, A.: *Tierleben.* Leipzig, 1896, 1911, 1914, 1924.

Cabrera, A.: "Catalogo de los mamiferos de America del Sur," *Revista Mus. Argent. Cienc. Nac. "Bernardino Rivadavia"*, Buenos Aires, 4: 1-732, 1957-1961.

Clarke, J. D. W.: *Modern Chinchilla Farming.* Toronto, 1961.

DeChant, C.J.: *Chinchilla Pelt and Herd Improvement.* Toronto, 1956.

Dellmann, H. D.: "Zur Anatomie der männichen Geschlechtsorgane der Chinchilla," *Zeitschr. Anat. Entwicklungsgesch.*, Berlin, 123: 137-154, 1962.

Desmarest, M. A. G.: *Mammalogie ou Description des Espèces des Mammifères.* Paris, 1820.

Foelsch, D.: "Zur makroskopischen und mikroskopischen Anatomie des Respirationsapparates der Chinchilla," *Säugetierk. Mitt.*, München, 14: 1-18, 1966.

Hodgson, R. G.: *Modern Chinchilla Pens and Equipment.* Toronto, 1956.

Houston, J. W. and Prestwich, J. P.: *Chinchilla Care.* Gardena, 1953.

Kaplan, H.: *Classifications of Fur-Bearing Animals.* London, 1948.

Kellogg, C. E.: *Chinchilla Raising.* Leaflet No. 266,

U.S. Department of Agriculture, Washington, D. C., 1950 and 1953.

Kraft, Dr. Helmut: *Krankheiten der Chinchillas*. München, 1974.

Lichtenstein, H.: *Darstellung neuerer oder wenig bekannter Säugethiere*. Berlin, 1827-1834.

Meyen, F. J.: *Beiträge zur Zoologie*. Breslau and Bonn, 1833.

Mösslacher, E.: *Die Chinchillazucht für jeden verständlich gemacht*. München, 1970.

Molina, I. G.: *Saggio sulla Storia Naturale del Chili*. Bologna, 1810.

Olborth, H.: "Zur Anatomie des Bewegungsapparates der Chinchillas," *Vet.-med. Diss.*, München, 1963.

Palmer, T. S: *Index Generum Mammalium*. Washington, D. C., 1904.

Parker, W. D.: *Chinchilla Farming in South Africa*. Pearston, 1961.

—: *Modern Chinchillas Farming*. Alhambra, California, 1975.

Poland, H.: *Fur Bearing Animals*. London, 1892.

Prell, H.: "Über die Benennung der Chinchilla-Arten und ihres Pelzwerkes," *Kleintier und Pelztier*, Leipzig, 10: 409-414, 1934.

Rosskopf, M.: *Zur Anatomie der Geschlechtsorgane der weiblichen Chinchilla*, Dissertation, München, 1961.

Schäuffelen, O.: "Zur Anatomie des Chinchillaschädels," *Veröff. Zool. Staatssammlung*, München, 5: 189-232, 1959.

Schreiber, G.: *Chinchilla-Pelzungsfibel*. München, 1966.

—: *Zuchtanleitung für Chinchillas*. München, 1975.

Schwab, G. R.: *Raising Chinchillas for Profit*. Toronto, 1949.

Shaul, E. M.: *Fur Quality and Fur-Breakage*. Santa Rosa, 1955.

Simon, N.: *Red Data Book, Vol. 1 — Mammalia*.

IUCN, Morges, 1966.

Taubert, J.: "Zur Anatomie der Chinchillazunge," *Tierärztl. Umschau, Konstanz,* 14: 125-127, 1959.

Trouessart, E.-L.: *Catalogues Mammalium tam vivantium quam fossilium.* Berlin, 1897 and 1904.

Tschudi, J. J.: *Fauna Peruana.* Berlin, 1844.

Waterhouse, G. R.: *A Natural History of the Mammalia.* London, 1848.

Index

224